NIGER:
JUST ANOTHER COUP
...OR A PAN-AFRICAN
REVOLUTION?

ALEX ANFRUNS MILLÁN

1804
books

Published in September 2024 by
1804 Books, New York, NY

1804Books.com

ISBN: 979-8-9910139-3-2
Library of Congress Control Number: 2024946869

Cover by Kael Abello

TABLE OF CONTENTS

ABOUT THE AUTHOR

Alex Anfruns Millán (Spain, 1980) is a journalist and coauthor of the collective book *Nicaragua: ¿Levantamiento popular o golpe de Estado?* (*Nicaragua: Popular Uprising or Coup?*), published in 2018, and of the 2008 Catalan documentary *Palestina: la verdad asediada* (*Palestine: The Truth Under Siege*). Formerly an editor at *Le Journal de Notre Amérique*, he was also chief editor of the Brussels-based website *Investig'Action* from 2014 to 2019. In collaboration with his Cameroonian colleague from Yaoundé, Olivier Ndenkop, he published the monthly magazine *Le journal de l'Afrique*, for four years. He has also translated and written about wars and coup attempts in Mali, Syria, Venezuela, and Nicaragua, focusing in particular on the histories of Africa and Latin America and the right to development. As a political analyst, he has appeared in media such as TeleSUR, RT Spanish, and Abya Yala TV. Having resided in Spain, France, and Belgium, he is currently a professor in Casablanca where his area of research is the right to development from a Pan-African historical perspective.

ACKNOWLEDGMENTS

I would like to thank and acknowledge:

My African, internationalist European and Latin American brothers and sisters to whom I am in debt for their constant inspiration and dedication to the causes of justice and peoples' liberation;

The fraternal peoples of Cuba and Venezuela for their heroic resistance in the face of the blockade and so-called sanctions, which are inhuman measures for the punishment of civilian populations solely comparable to fascist methods;

The beloved Latin American peoples of Abya Yala (Our America) in struggle against oppression and for a more just and beautiful future for their children;

The Palestinian people for their fortitude and resistance in the face of the neo-fascist occupation of their land; and

My comrades—social movement activists and intellectuals—of the Network for the Defense of Humanity.

"Without international solidarity, without the support rendered to our workers' resolute struggle by their class brothers from the entire world and especially from the admirable people of the Soviet Union, in the face of a powerful, unscrupulous, and aggressive imperialism, the virtual lord and master of the destinies of the peoples of this hemisphere, Cuban revolutionaries might have died heroically, like the Communards of Paris, but without tasting victory."

— *Fidel Castro*

"It's time for the United States and Europe to learn from experience . . . For thirteen years, we've launched one military intervention after another (Afghanistan, Iraq, Libya, and Mali). In 2001, the terrorist crisis was confined to a single hot spot. Today, there's close to fifteen of them. In other words, terrorism has proliferated because of us. And to what end? That is *the* question because, today, the Islamic State is the monstrous offspring of Western policy, of its fickleness and arrogance."

— *Dominique de Villepin,*
Former French Foreign Minister,
during an interview on French television,
in September 2014

INTRODUCTION

Niger has a population of twenty-seven million, ten million of whom live in extreme poverty. Only one in three Nigeriens is literate and, worse still, just one woman in six can read and write.[1] Moreover, early school dropout is an issue that directly affects Niger's fertility rate, which, at 6.68 live births per woman (in 2023), is the world's highest. Consequently, Niger has one of the world's youngest populations.

Furthermore, Africans from many other countries live in Niger as refugees in flight from terrorism, including Senegalese people, Burkinabe, sixty-one thousand Malians, and two hundred thousand Nigerians. The terrorism of the Boko Haram group, which also operates in Cameroon, Nigeria, Chad, and Mali, has provoked the internal displacement of 264,000 persons from southeastern and western Niger since 2015.[2] According to Dominique Hyde, Director of External Relations for the UN High Commission for Refugees, Niger is a *generous country that maintains open borders and welcomes refugees*,[3] despite being the fourth-poorest country in the world.[4] Niger shares a 1,500 km border with Nigeria, its neighbor to the south.

Niger has a rural economy and 80 percent of its population live in rural areas. Major cross-border trade takes place between Benin, Nigeria, and Niger. As a result, many families and workers live on either side of these borders.[5] Niger has a large trade deficit: its average annual exports total a little over €1 billion compared to average annual imports of €2.3 billion. According to the African Development Bank, in 2022, Niger's public debt was equal to 51.2 percent of its Gross Domestic Product, i.e., half the value of the country's goods and services.[6] In December 2005, Niger's multilateral International Monetary Fund (IMF) debt was canceled. However, as the debt forgiven totaled a mere $86 million, this debt relief had little practical effect. In comparison, after former Nigerien president Mohamed Bazoum was deposed, Prime Minister Lamine Zeine of the transition government estimated that Niger had a combined public and external debt of €8 billion.

Niger is being asked to service its foreign debt with payments equal to four times the value of its imports, even though 37 percent of its population lives in extreme poverty![*] Is that even possible, and if so, how? Some take comfort in the illusory belief that the country's mineral resources will drive the country's economic growth. To assess the validity of that view, one needs to take a close look at export policies and analyze the commercial terms under which different trade agreements were signed. Others, namely international creditors, seem anxious to ensure that nothing changes. In effect, two weeks after Bazoum's removal from power by the National Council for Safeguarding the Homeland (*Conseil national pour la*

---

*   [Editor's Note: The percentage of the population expected to live in extreme poverty was expected to reach 52 percent by 2023 according to the World Bank.]

sauvegarde de la patrie—CNSP), creditors issued warnings on July 26, 2023, concerning the coup government's inability to make debt service payments in the amount of 70 billion CFA francs by the upcoming deadlines in August and September. The mind boggles! Those who had so kindly made loans to Niger are unconcerned about the survival of a population confronted by food shortages due to sanctions imposed by the European Union (EU) and the Economic Community of West African States (ECOWAS). No, their sole concern is that debt payments be made on time! How legitimate is debt repayment in African countries? In 1987, shortly before his death, President Thomas Sankara of Burkina Faso gave a speech in which he called the debt an instrument of neocolonialism and invited the African Union to form a united front to renounce repayment of the debt:

> The debt cannot be repaid because, first of all, if we don't repay it, our creditors will not die. That is certain. However, if we do repay it, we are going to die. That too is certain. Those who led us into indebtedness gambled as if they were in a casino. As long as they were winning there was no issue, but now that they're suffering losses, they demand repayment and speak of the debt crisis. No, Mr. President, they gambled and they lost. That's how the game works.[7]

Since the intervention of a group of nationalist soldiers from the CNSP which deposed Bazoum and the rapid designation of a transition government, the situation has changed dramatically. ECOWAS has demonstrated that it is an instrument in the service of France and the United

States. In effect, rather than calm tensions and seek a diplomatic solution, it has instead increased tensions, imposed economic sanctions and declared war on Niger. As for Western leaders, they have made it very clear they believe Niger's resources belong to them and are ready to create a humanitarian crisis in order to justify a military intervention. Thus, according to Emanuela Del Re, the EU's Special Representative for the Sahel, sanctions, which cause shortages in medicines, food, and electricity, are useful and effective for weakening the junta in power. In other words, to be blunt, she couldn't care less about the Nigerien people's suffering.

Thanks to the change in government, the Nigerien people now know who its enemies are. As media propaganda would have it, the French military's presence is necessary to combat terrorism in Niger. And yet, at the same time, hasn't the very same media brazenly declared war on the new authorities? This means that Niger's transition government faces the prospect of fighting on several fronts at once, i.e., against terrorist groups and against foreign invaders, either in the form of French troops or an ECOWAS African coalition.[8] Should that happen, there'd be no room for doubt: France would be the objective ally of the terrorists. Does the French Army (or its Senegalese or Ivoirian auxiliaries) mean to suggest that it knows the national territory of Niger better than the Nigerien Army? If France is acting this way, it's because of its long history of alternately overthrowing its African allies or restoring them to power.

The struggle over access to African raw materials remains the key to understanding the continent's problems. In Africa, national economies are based on export revenues. This economic model puts African countries in a situation of dependence and has failed to resolve the problem of extreme poverty. What if an African country diversified its economic partners? Would that suffice? Would it suffice to renegotiate mining and resource extraction policies? What mortal traps will the neocolonial powers lay?

What this little book proposes to do is to serve as a quick guide for analyzing how the transition governments of West Africa (i.e., the former colonies of the French West Africa Federation of 1895–1958) can overcome contemporary obstacles by transforming how their resources are used to the benefit of their populations.

From 2014 to 2019, I published *Le journal de l'Afrique* in collaboration with my colleague, the Cameroonian journalist Olivier Ndenkop. We analyzed the background to the current crises, in particular, the decline of the *Françafrique* system, the causes and limits of French military strategies, and the rebirth of Pan-Africanism among the younger generations. Political developments in subsequent years have brought to fruition the hope that glimmered in popular struggles. Later, as an independent journalist, I interviewed experts and African political figures. This was an eye-opening experience as someone who has focused on following current events in Latin America, which deepened my grasp of Africa's problems and challenges. The processes of change in twenty-first-century Latin America offer many lessons for Africa: in effect, in a continent like Africa, it's not enough to gain political freedom from neocolonial tutelage. Africa's economic development projects must adopt the correct approach by banking on the strategic sectors historically offered on a platter to the former colonial powers. The point is not to turn these sectors over to new masters, but to benefit the peoples of Africa.

In that regard, one can draw lessons from the Global South's own history in the twentieth century regarding the advances and limitations characteristic of societies governed by regimes that emerged after military coups, such as the governments of Gamal Abdul Nasser in Egypt or Juan Velasco Alvarado in Peru.

The case of Hugo Chávez, who restored participatory democracy to his country after a failed coup in 1992, may be seen as an exception to the rule. One of Chávez' primary objectives, as the leader of a founding member of OPEC (the Organization of the Petroleum Exporting Countries), was to develop ties of solidarity among countries of the Global South in order to found a multipolar world. Once he had consolidated popular power, i.e., after the people had defeated the April 2002 coup attempt, Chávez turned to fighting the structures of corruption embedded in the *Magical State* that had emerged out of the oil boom early in the twentieth century. The goal was to supplant the bourgeois rentier state with the new social structures of the *Communal State*. This experience of struggle remains at the center of the current challenges in Venezuela and Latin America. Thus, it's possible that the objective of the system of unilateral sanctions and the blockade imposed by the US goes beyond regime change by fomenting popular discontent. It's also a matter of destroying the relevance of the socialist offensive emerging from the Bolivarian Republic of Venezuela.

With the wars in Syria and Ukraine, recourse to the sanctions weapon has become ubiquitous. As a result, more and more peoples, especially in Africa, are coming to understand that the United States and its allies do not seek to foster democracy or human rights. On the contrary, their objective is to punish with inhuman cruelty the peoples and governments who struggle and resist and who are building the new multipolar world. They have no other choice: it's a life and death struggle. The alternative, which is very real, is based on human development, in which peoples have access to food, employment, housing, health, and education up to the university level. Those who consider this utopian are, in a sense, right: it is utopian as long as we are in the midst of a multifaceted war that imperialism wages against any independent socialist or popular experiment escaping its clutches. For capitalists, it would be a nightmare if the countries of the Global South were able to stop the brain drain and independently develop their own industry and technology as sovereign countries. This other world is possible, but it demands the perseverance, will, and discipline to fight back . . .

Fortunately, today's Pan-African generation has clear ideological reference points: Thomas Sankara, Kwame Nkrumah, and Muammar Qadafi are remembered as the precursors and heralds of contemporary processes. As for the nationalist militaries in Mali, Burkina Faso, and Niger, they've taken a noble and decisive step by confronting the Western powers as a united front. *If they touch Niger, it will be a declaration of war on us as well!* This extremely positive message has lifted the morale and dignity of millions of Africans. As for the path they ultimately choose and the future success of their enterprise, that will depend on their political maturity and on how close they are to their peoples whose daily problems must serve to guide their actions and self-criticism.

CHAPTER 1

FROM THE FRENCH INTERVENTION IN MALI TO THE COUP IN NIGER

It's August 2023, and the face of the African continent is changing along the length and breadth of the Sahel, from the Atlantic Ocean to the Indian Ocean. The Sahel is a region shared by over 320 million inhabitants of different nations that affirmed their place in the sun during the era of African independence in the 1960s. Today, however, African states are still struggling to escape the spiral of dependence on the former colonial powers.

This desire for autonomy has led to regime changes, which put nationalist military officers in power in four countries: Mali, on August 18, 2020; Guinea, on September 5, 2021; Burkina Faso, on September 30, 2022; and Niger, on July 26, 2023. With the exception of Guinea, these leaders have above all expressed their firm rejection of the interventionist policies of France, the former colonial power. It is that stance that is behind the recent expulsion of French troops from the republics of Mali and Burkina Faso.

In response, ECOWAS suspended the membership of all four countries—Burkina Faso, Guinea, Mali, and Niger—and implemented punitive measures, including the freezing of financial assets, the imposing of economic and financial sanctions, and the suspension of business transactions. The objectives are clear: isolate countries that demand control over their natural resources and asphyxiate and inflict exemplary suffering on populations who support governments that have escaped the West's sphere of influence.

Consequently, these nationalist military officers see ECOWAS as an instrument of domination in the service of neocolonial interests—attested by its inability or unwillingness to modernize the monetary system, which is based on the CFA franc, the former colonial currency unit. In the face of growing demonstrations against the continuing use of the CFA franc, which Africans see as a symbol of servility, ECOWAS had expressed an intention to introduce a regional money named the "eco." Events have led many to wonder: What is the true purpose of ECOWAS? Does it exist to build regional integration or to keep the Sahel divided?

Immediately following the creation of the newly independent states, nationalist leaders and the founding fathers of the Pan-African struggle analyzed and enunciated the risks in store for future generations, who would not have direct knowledge of colonialism, except via neocolonial mechanisms. That political program was present in the social struggles of African peoples for decades. Until recently, all of these countries remained subject to different forms of neocolonial tutelage. It wasn't until the sixtieth anniversary of independence that this struggle crystallized in the form of a wave of nationalist military uprisings. Shortly before addressing the UN General Assembly on September 25, 2021, Choguel Kokalla, prime minister of Mali's transition government, summarized the problem as follows:

> One cannot prohibit us from buying goods from a certain country, if we have concluded an agreement with it, merely because another country is opposed. We must have the opportunity to look towards other horizons, as this broadens our possibilities for cooperation in the interests of our national defense.[9]

Kokalla concluded by denouncing France for having abandoned Mali "in mid-flight." In response, French president Emmanuel Macron declared the following:

> It's unacceptable . . . It's a disgrace and dishonors what is not even a government . . . [what] is the offspring of two coups . . . [10] We are there at the request of the Malian State. Without France, Mali would be in the hands of terrorists.

Who's right and who's wrong? Let's find out by taking a close look at events.

Officially, the purpose of the French military presence in the Sahel was to carry out joint military interventions in accordance with a regional security agreement. Operation Serval, which commenced in 2013 with the French intervention in Mali, expanded when it became Operation Barkhane on August 1, 2014, with a planned field of operation in the Sahel and the Sahara. In February 2014, France and five states—Mauritania, Mali, Burkina Faso, Niger, and Chad—signed a development and security policies agreement known as the G5S (G5 Sahel). Did this represent a balanced and equal relationship? Not in the least, due to France's paternalist attitude and tendency to see these countries (its former colonies) as fragile or failed states, incapable of dispensing with foreign support.

On February 13, 2020, the G5S Summit—held meaningfully in Pau, France, i.e., in the former colonial power—decided to increase the French military contingent to five thousand soldiers, in the face of alarming signs of growing insecurity in the Sahel. Shortly thereafter, a new series of Islamist attacks occurred in Sokolo and Ogossagou (Mali); in Silgadji, Yagha, and Nagraogo (Burkina Faso); and in Chinégodar and Tillabéry (Niger). Following these events, a group of African intellectuals—including notably Aminata Traoré, the former Malian Minister of Culture—refuted the humiliating notion of failed states in the Sahel, by publishing the following denunciation:

> . . . all the other localities martyred by this cursed anti-terrorist war are only plots of a global world on fire (. . .) The G5 Sahel states, weakened by the structural adjustment programs of the Bretton Woods institutions and the laws of the capitalist market, are also suffering the consequences of the attack on Libya. (. . .) two major pitfalls obstruct the horizon: on the one hand, the refusal to recognize the real causes of "jihadism" and migrations, namely neoliberalism and its ravages, and on the other, the gagging of our people.[11]

Demonstrating a Pan-African political outlook, the peoples of Africa have denounced the French troops stationed in their countries as an army of occupation that violates the principle of national sovereignty. This presence became increasingly unpopular as year after year passed without bringing any definitive solution to the problem of terrorism. According to French investigative reporter Bruno Jaffré: "The massive shift in opinion against France was essentially due to the absence of results after seven or eight years of the French military presence and interventions."[12] Among the examples of mistrust and hostility in Franco-Burkinabé relations, Jaffré mentions "the statements of Cherif Sy, then the new Minister of Defense, who accused France of blocking arms shipments to ports in West Africa."[13] As for the tensions in Franco-Malian relations, Jaffré underlines an "event that provoked strong feelings of hostility among Malians, which persist to this day," namely "the time French troops prevented the Malian army from entering into Kidal," a city then under the control of terrorist groups.

In February 2020, the Malian army returned to retake control of Kidal, thereby ending the splintering of the country that dated back to 2013. This deployment of the Malian army to regain control of sovereign territory was a provision of the 2015 Peace Agreement (officially the Agreement for Peace and Reconciliation in Mali) signed in Algiers. Said peace agreement also provided for the integration into the National Army of those armed groups that are signatories to the agreement, such as the Coordinator of Azawad Movements (*Coordination des mouvements de l'Azawad*—CMA). Regarding the Malian government's recovery of Kidal, Sahel Studies scholar Yvan Guichaoua confirmed that the national army was relegated to a secondary role: this long-awaited return "was conducted under the protection of international forces, which is quite paradoxical!"[14]

On the one hand, Operation Serval in Mali was approved by the interim Malian government of Dioncounda Traoré, after the AQIM (al-Qaeda in the Islamic Maghreb) Islamists had gained the upper hand against the Tuareg rebels and threatened to take the capital, Bamako. However, Mali's initial request for assistance did not include the deployment of land forces. Moreover, from the point of view of democratic norms, it's doubtful whether France could take such a dangerous and unpopular decision as that of sending troops abroad without the approval of its National Assembly. Moreover, the rebel uprising also awoke nationalist sentiments among sectors of the military, which, on behalf of the National Committee for the Recovery of Democracy and the Restoration of the State (*Comité national pour le redressement de la démocratie et la restauration de l'État*—CNRDR), carried out a coup on March 22, 2012. The rebels accused the government of Amadou Toumani Touré of having failed to "provide the armed forces with the means necessary to defend the integrity of our national territory."

Meanwhile, the double dealing of the Tuareg independence movement was a major factor in prolonging the conflict with the Malian state. Guichaoua highlights the historical underpinnings of this movement's demands:

> … there's no reason to expect the population to applaud the arrival of the national security forces in Kidal. People have mixed memories of the [Malian] army. Its original sin was the repression of the first Tuareg rebellion in 1963, an event still very much alive in people's memories.[15]

This background explains why the Azawad National Liberation Movement (MNLA) proclaimed "the Independent State of Azawad," shortly after it took Timbuktu. Although the European Union and France both officially rejected this declaration of independence, Paris offered the MNLA its continuous support; and did so despite documented evidence of relations between the MNLA and Islamist groups such as Ansar Dine, another terrorist group in the Sahel.

This was confirmed by none other than the general and French army's chief of staff of the military operation Barkhane, who made the following statement during a press conference on November 21, 2017:

> There are armed groups in northern Mali, which, despite being signatories to the Peace and Reconciliation Accord, have one foot in the Accord and another in terrorist groups. Today, we have material evidence of this collusion.[16]

France's so-called "anti-terrorist struggle" is shot through with contradictions. Moreover, in light of the four thousand lives taken by Islamist attacks in Mali, Burkina Faso, and Niger in 2019 alone,[17] it must be deemed ineffective as well. And yet, some appear to dismiss this record of failure. "What's the difference?" they retort. Nor, it would appear, do these failed military operations trouble French General François Lecointre, chief of staff of the imperialist army. According to Lecointre, the French army's presence should be maintained until at least around the year 2050:

> We are here to ensure our security for the next thirty years (. . .) because if we allow chaos to reign the states of the Sahel will collapse and open space for the Islamic State, thereby provoking migratory pressures towards Europe, with all the risks of populism that would bring.[18]

Perhaps the key word in these frank remarks is the term "our security." So, what type of security do you mean General Lecointre? Is it the security provided by the border between the "garden and the jungle," as Josep Borell, the European Union's chief diplomat, cynically put it? Obviously, but truth be told, the European Union's border security has in fact been "outsourced" to several non-EU countries, such as Tunisia and Turkey, which the EU is happy to shower with millions of euros. In so doing, the EU throws a veil over media coverage of its responsibilities in the Mediterranean. Or was General Lecointre perhaps referring to Europe's energy security?

During the crisis provoked by the advancing Tuareg secessionists, Mali's president, A. Toumani Touré, acknowledged that his country had been destabilized by the 2011 NATO intervention in Libya:

> Mali is suffering the collateral effects of the war in Libya, which has become the biggest, cheapest and best supplied open-air arms market in the world. After the fall of Qadafi's regime, people of Malian origin or nationality, and who had fought on the side of the former regime, returned to the country of their ancestors with their suitcases and weapons.[19]

In January 2012, the foreign ministers of Mauritania, Mali, Niger, and Algeria met to discuss the security situation in the Sahel. In July 2012, the Ansar Dine Islamists destroyed the seven Timbuktu mausoleums. Subsequently, the destruction of these UNESCO world heritage sites was often mentioned in pro-war propaganda intended to justify a military intervention. Hama Ag

Mamoud, the MNLA's former head of Foreign Affairs, outlined how the intervention in Libya was connected with the war in Mali in his account of the agreements between the MNLA and France:

> France asked the MNLA to help it by encouraging all Tuareg combatants who were in the Libyan army during the war in Libya to desert and also by blocking the recruitment of Libyans in northern Mali and in the Äir Mountains in Niger. In return, France greenlighted Azawad's independence. This was the agreement we concluded with France.[20]

The denouement to this tangle of neocolonial intriguing came in May 2022 when Mali announced its withdrawal from the G5S and on November 9, 2022, when Paris opted for the permanent withdrawal of its troops from Malian territory. Meanwhile, the French interventions in Libya and Mali also had the effect of destabilizing neighboring countries through the migration crisis in the Mediterranean, which transformed the latter into a marine cemetery. Among the terrible consequences was the displacement of Malian refugees to Niger and the shameful way in which Europe delegated its antimigration policies to the countries of North Africa. The consequences of those policy decisions hit rock bottom with the return of African slave markets in Libya. According to the 2022 Global Report of the United Nations High Commission on Refugees, "the deteriorating security situation and the escalation of the conflict in the Sahel led to an increase in the forcibly displaced population,"[21] which rose by a half a million persons between 2021 and 2022 and reached a total of 4.1 million.

On August 3, 2023, the National Council for Safe-guarding the Homeland (CNSP) announced the cancellation of Niger's military agreements and protocols with France. This decision heightened tensions in the extreme, thereby raising the threat of a regional war with incalculable consequences. According to French Foreign Minister Catherine Colonna, this was "one coup too many." The minister also called the recourse to force by ECOWAS a "credible threat." For France, West Africa's former colonial master, it's preferable when it's an African organization that issues an ultimatum and threatens military intervention, as that provides a veneer of neutrality. However, haste is a poor counselor. That, along with Colonna's irrepressible love of the limelight, led her to announce: "the authors of the coup have until tomorrow to renounce their adventurism." Why such an uproar, if these were, as the rebels had clearly stated, "transition governments"?

The African militaries that carried out nationalist coups between 2020 and 2023 have promised to organize elections in or around 2024. Captain Ibrahim Traoré of Burkina Faso has said that he wasn't there to take power, that he wanted civilians to choose their president and that the timeline promised would be respected. Colonel Assimi Goita in Mali has expressed the same intentions. This adherence to democratic elections may be a double-edged sword. Arguments in favor of a rapid return to the constitutional order are illusory. If it were enough to simply approve a new constitution or put new faces in power, there would have been no need to take such great risks; in reality, the fundamental issue is to "refound" the nation per se. This is why ECOWAS, Paris, and Washington want "their president" back in power. They know that if elections were held after a civilian-military transition that that would leave their pawns on the sidelines. To the extent that the transition governments respond to the demands of their peoples, the Western powers are right to be worried. In the streets of Niamey, Bamako, and Ouagadou, people are chanting: "Down with France! Down with imperialism! No more foreign military bases!" Today, there are governments that are acting decisively to turn these slogans into policy, in a full-fledged attack on neocolonialism!

That being said, one must not confuse mere political statements with real decolonization. Decolonization is a new, post-independence, process of struggle. Cultural and economic decolonization is a laborious task, as nationalist soldiers and Pan-African revolutionaries well know, one which is partially motivated by their rejection of corruption. So, let's suppose they take a step back and trust in the election of a popular leader or legitimate political party. How, in that scenario, would they be able to avoid a resurgence of corruption? How could they avoid the reversal of the military government's decisions that were to the peoples' benefit?

In the 1960s, the countries of the Global South put their right to development on the world agenda through higher prices for their natural resources. What, in the end, were the results of those demands? Moreover, why is this coup not like the others, but rather "one coup too many"? In answering that question, one needs to consider Niger's strategic role from the standpoint of the Western powers. Niger's position as the world's seventh-largest uranium producer may have a lot to do with France's concerns and its frenzied interventionism.[22]

Facts speak louder than words. Thus, what underlies the solid support enjoyed by the military rebellions in Africa is the moral courage demonstrated by their leaders. By stating its firm intention to wage a dual struggle against imperialism and corruption, the junta in Niger has gained the support of broad sectors of the population, including students' and teachers' unions. That said, they are subject to all kinds of pressure and intimidation. Consequently, it is to be expected that would-be turncoats will emerge from within the ranks of the military, particularly since some officers were trained in American or French military schools. For some, rebellion against Paris may be a way to assert their independence. Alternatively, such rebellions may in fact be evidence that the United States is craftier in how it wins friends and influences partners to gain adherence to its interests.

A third option would to be more overt in expressing their sovereignty in the face of Washington's demands, in which case they would be defying hegemony and actively participating in a new world order, one in which African countries would have greater latitude when negotiating new contracts, whether it be with the old colonial powers or with BRICS countries. Conclusion: it is only when the Pan-African movement consolidates economically and African leaders act as the political instruments of their peoples will Africa be able to resist attacks, interference, and military interventions.

CHAPTER 2

THE ERRORS OF FRENCH INTERFERENCE IN THE SAHEL

In general, the countries that gained their independence in the 1960s were "granted" that status, under conditions set by France. As a consequence, said countries maintained ties of neocolonial domination, either through their currency, the CFA franc, or in the form of economic, cooperation, and security agreements. It's quite illuminating to read the 1960–1961 Defense Agreements signed by France and the new states: " . . . the contracting parties hereby decide to cooperate in the realm of the following defense-related materials: liquid and gaseous hydrocarbons, uranium, thorium, lithium, beryllium, and the ores and compounds thereof."[23]

Historian Thomas Deltombe clarifies the curious concept of capitalist "cooperation." Such cooperation is a one-way street, in which the African Republics "shall prioritize sales to the French Republic" and "when defense interests so require, they shall limit or prohibit their exports to third countries."[24]

In many of the new republics, nationalist and revolutionary leaders continued the anti-colonial struggle by denouncing this nominal and false independence. The response was repression, jailings, and extra-judicial assassinations, such as in the case of Sylvanus Olympio, Togo's first president whose mandate was terminated with extreme prejudice, with the active participation of the French ambassador, as attests the recent research of historian Adovi Michel Goeh Akué. In effect, after a commando attack on his residence, Olympio sought and—believed he found—refuge in the nearby American embassy. However, his executioners were able to locate him thanks to a conversation between the US ambassador and his French opposite number[25] who then betrayed Olympio in a phone call to said executioners. Goeh Akué finds it deplorable that even sixty years later, detailed information on these events remains confidential due to the refusal to open French military archives. It is, however, a known fact that the commando unit responsible for Olympio's assassination had acquired experience in the art of killing during the colonial wars in Indochina and Algeria.

Similarly, the repression suffered by the Diop brothers in Senegal, accused of having claimed responsibility for setting fire to the French Cultural Center in Dakar and of throwing Molotov cocktails during French president Georges Pompidou's first visit to their country, shows how young Senegalese who protested against neocolonialism paid a high price for their actions. The arson of a site symbolic of the French presence in Africa presaged today's attacks on French embassies and cultural and education centers.

Although African youth of the twenty-first century may not have the same political culture as the independence generation of the 1960s, like causes do generate like effects. Thus, French officials watched the attack on their embassy in Niamey with horror. One wonders, however: are they just as indignant about the radioactive contamination in areas where the multinational

Orano (formerly known as Areva) mines uranium? Do they wonder whether the low life expectancy of Nigeriens might somehow be connected with the preservation of an economic system which essentially favors France? Do they know or care about Niger's recent history, marked by the failure of a development plan elaborated under IMF tutelage, in accordance with neoliberal principles? Does the fact that public spending on defense and security (10 percent of the national budget) exceed the combined spending on health and education (at 5.7 percent and 3.8 percent, respectively) make any impression on them?

What was not possible in the past, may become possible once all of the agreements entrenching submission to the former colonial power are broken and all foreign military bases sent packing. It is this sense that Mali, Burkina Faso, and Niger represent the vanguard of the Pan-African revolution.

What actually happened? How was France dealt such an historic reversal of fortune? French neocolonialism appears not to have drawn lessons from the defeats suffered by its colonial empire. Whether it's the policy of supporting and allying with the most conservative sectors of society, or the policy of "divide and rule" through support for ethnic groups with secessionist designs, or the advancing of some legitimizing ideology to justify their presence and control over their colonial possessions, none of these strategies functioned as expected.

Under the colonial system, French schools sought to educate an indigenous elite, who would adopt and share the values of "French civilization" and thereby better defend the interests of colonialism. At the same time, the great majority of the indigenous population was excluded from access to education, as was quite apparent in the policies of the French Protectorate in Morocco. This was acknowledged by two members of the Colonial Academy of Sciences, Roger Coindreau and Charles Penz, who observed:

> From the point of view of Moroccan nationalists, France has done nothing in the Muslim education sector (. . .) Let's immediately acknowledge that the statistics appear do substantially support this argument. After thirty-six years of Protectorate governance, the proportion of educated Muslim youth is tiny: 110,000 in 1947 out of a school-age population of over a million.[26]

In the event, the procolonial education of African elites did not prevent them from turning into colonialism's worst enemy as the leaders of nationalist movements and the anti-colonial resistance:

> As the American historian Frederick Cooper explains, in the 1930s, various political movements, which were not purely local or national, germinated in the ferment of the post-war period. When intellectuals from the colonies toured great European capitals, the effect produced was the opposite of the objective sought by "indigenous administration" policy. For example, when Hồ Chí Minh traveled from Vietnam to Paris, he met people from throughout the empire as well as French communists. His tour subsequently took him to Moscow and then China before he returned to Vietnam, where he would soon launch a revolutionary movement. George Padmore left Trinidad for London,

Moscow, and later, the Gold Coast (as Ghana was then known). He played an important if interim role in the Comintern. However, disappointed with the limited Communist support for the cause of Africa, he moved on and became an eminent figure in radical Pan-African organizations in the late 1930s and the 1940s. In 1945, he played an especially prominent role at the Manchester Pan-African Conference, where he crossed paths with figures like W. E. B. Dubois, Kwame Nkrumah, and Jomo Kenyatta.[27]

The experience of fighting in the Second World War awoke nationalist sentiments among many African combatants from the colonies, along with a clear understanding that the white man could be defeated. So great was this political awakening that France, mired in wars in Algeria and Indochina, decided to renounce its colonial empire. In the case of the former French West Africa (*Afrique-Occidentale française*—AOF), however, France attempted to carry on with its instruments of colonial control, sometimes obtaining adverse results, as Frederick Cooper observes in relation to Mali (the former French Sudan):

> In the AOF, attempts to breathe new life into the highly intrusive Niger Office—which was tasked with developing rice and cotton cultivation in French Sudan—provoked issues around which the Sudanese sections of the Democratic African Assembly (*Rassemblement démocratique africain*—RDA) succeeded in organizing rural populations. African parties like the RDA could rightly

affirm that—in contrast with colonial notables—they alone could ensure that development projects would be administered in the interests of local African populations rather than used to intensify colonial exploitation. However, in places where funding for development made it possible to obtain new resources, such as in Nigeria, intense rivalries sometimes arose between different regions and ethnic groups for access to these riches.[28]

Jean Ramadier, who succeeded Pierre Messmer as High Commissioner of the colonies in the AOF, first gained notoriety as the Governor of Niger and Guinea from 1954 to 1958. It was during his mandate in these two countries that the nationalist movements led by the Guinean Sékou Touré and the Nigerien Djibo Bakary emerged. Confronted with the reality of these anti-colonial movements, Ramadier broke a taboo by being the first to publicly allude to the question of independence for the colonies when he revealed a secret French strategy, practiced by Yaoundé High Commissioner Daniel Doustin. In his memoirs, Doustin explained his doctrine as follows: "France shall grant independence to those who are the least militant in demanding it, after having politically and militarily eliminated those who are the most uncompromising in demanding it."[29] Paris lost no time in meting out its punishment for this indiscretion: Ramadier held his post in Cameroon for a mere fifteen days.

In Niger, Bakary left the Nigerien Progressive Party in 1954 to found the Nigerien Democratic Union (UDN). On the eve of the September 28, 1958 referendum on the proposed French Community in Africa and Madagascar,

Bakary set the goal of obtaining the same result as his fraternal comrade Touré in Guinea, where the "No" side won with 95 percent of the votes. As president of the Nigerien Council and leader of the Sawaba movement (*Union des Forces Populaires pour la Démocratie et le Progrès – Sawaba*), Bakary denounced the territorial fragmentation implied in the De Gaulle plan, which he labeled as "steeped in imperialism." Bakary likewise rejected the economic blackmail and hypocrisy of FIDES.[30] As a delegate at the meeting of the African Regroupment Party (*Parti du regroupement africain*—PRA), held in Cotonou in July 1957, Bakary put Senghor in the minority when he gained the support of the majority of delegates by pointing out that "Niger receives less funding than Gabon, which has a smaller population but exports oil."[31]

However, as historian Thomas Deltombe explains, in Niamey, "the coalition government collapsed under the unrelenting pressure of the French administration, which engineered a comfortable victory for the 'Yes' side through a rigged vote and forced the inconvenient leader to resign."[32] According to historian Klaas van Walraven, circles close to French businessman Jacques Foccart were behind the "injection of large sums of money into the Yes campaign, along with vehicles and personnel—including both armed men and advisors (. . .) The French Army transferred forces from Algiers to Niamey to terrorize the population in Sawaba's electoral strongholds." As a result, nearly forty thousand terrorized peasants fled to Nigeria.[33] Sawaba the party gave way to Sawaba the armed guerilla movement, active from 1960 to 1966. Have the Nigerien people forgotten the terrorism of the colonial state, that is to say the predecessor of today's terrorism?

Doustin's strategy was successfully applied in the countries where nationalist leaders were the least "intransigent." In 1982, Jean Ziegler denounced the installation of the dictatorship of Ahmadou Adhidjo in Cameroon:

> . . . by the French government and large colonial businesses. His secret services assassinated all of the UPC's [*Union des populations du Cameroun*] leaders, one by one. Ruben Um Nyobé, the founder of the movement and the one who launched the insurrection of 1955, was assassinated. Also killed were his aides Nyobé Pandjok, David Mitton, and Tankeu Noté. On October 14, it was Félix-Roland Moumié's turn. Moumié, then leader of the UPC, had come to Geneva to obtain arms. A "journalist" with UN accreditation invited him to lunch. That evening, Moumié felt intense stomach pains (. . .) and died in the night. This "journalist" was rapidly identified as one William Bechtel, an SDECE [*Service de documentation extérieure et de contre-espionnage* (External Documentation and Counter-Espionage Service)] official, and an international arrest warrant was issued. Twenty years later, on December 8, 1980, the Chamber of Indictments in Geneva found in favor of Bechtel and dismissed the case.[34]

To Ziegler's surprise, this verdict practically coincided with the revelations published just a week earlier by a certain Colonel Le Roy-Finville. In his memoirs, the colonel, who in 1960 was none other than Bechtel's boss, described in detail the assassination of Moumié in Geneva by his employee on November 3, 1960.

Another non-African actor has played a role in interference in the former French colonies. Thomas Deltombe describes how

> ... effectively, since the early 1960s, the Israeli government has developed ambitious military, agricultural, and educational assistance programs aimed at sub-Saharan Africa, which are designed as complementary programs. In Niger, for example, the Israelis were active in the retraining of soldiers demobilized by the French army who had served in Algeria.[35]

The situation in the current period is quite different: today, many high-ranking African officers have also been trained in American or French military schools and, upon returning to their countries, were supposed to place themselves under the command of foreign advisors. Millions of dollars have been allocated to cooperation and security programs without producing the slightest glimmer of a solution to the terrorism problem.

With the exception of the "uranium boom" in the second half of the 1970s, income from this commodity has not enabled the construction of schools, hospitals, or public infrastructure. Nor has it increased Nigeriens' life expectancy. As a result, just as with the previous generation of anti-colonial patriots after the Second World War, certain sectors of the military have, in response, sought to realize their patriotic ideal of sovereignty. In any case, President Mohamed Bazoum did not trust Chief of Staff of the Armed Forces, General Salifou Mody. According to Rahmane Idrissa,[36] Bazoum may have had wind of the imminent CNSP coup. This would explain why he dismissed Mody from his post on April 1, 2023, and, two months later, named him ambassador to the United Emirates "a potential source of lucrative gains."

After the coup, Mody, as vice president of the CNSP and its second-highest-ranking leader, was rapidly dispatched to Bamako to negotiate collective security measures. Bazoum, who was Interior Minister under Mahmadou Issoufou, could be seen as having followed in the latter's footsteps, i.e., to have acted as a president in the service of foreign interests. According to Idrissa, the Issoufou government's program of social spending entailed minimizing spending on security. That, however, was only feasible "if Issoufou decided to seek the help of the West assistance to contain the fallout" from the region's security and migration crisis, which came in the wake of the war in Libya.[37] However, a qualitative leap had taken place inasmuch as the current generation of patriotic military officers were not ex-combatants under a colonial protectorate, but rather active military officers with experience in defending their nation's sovereignty and, consequently, capable of accomplishing the historic mission of State building.

The events in Mali, Burkina Faso, and Niger represent a clear setback for imperialism, one arising from a paternalist and arrogant tradition flatly rejected by the new African leaders. That, however, does not mean that private interests in France have surrendered. Foreign Minister Colonna has repeatedly raised the threat of a French military intervention in support of ECOWAS forces in Niger. The media in France denounce the "scandalous" attack on the French embassy and the demonstrations just outside the French military base in Niamey. What did they expect? The French military presence is no longer seen as assistance and popular discontent in Niger simply reflects the extent of foreign interference. Bloody terrorist attacks have exposed the failure of what was supposedly a short-term operation and raised suspicions that insecurity is here to stay.[38]

In December 2019, seventy-one Malian soldiers died as a result of a terrorist attack in the tri-border region with Mali and Burkina Faso, an area that has known no respite. A few days later, on January 9, 2020, eighty-nine more soldiers were killed during an attack on the Chinégodar military camp. A year later, during the interval between the two rounds of the presidential election, about one hundred persons were killed in Mangaizé. In March 2021, the Nigerien region of Tahoua, to the east of Tillabéri, was the scene of a massacre of sixty-six inhabitants and the criminal destruction of a grain warehouse. The same day, another attack, this time against soldiers, killed thirty-three. In a single week, nearly two hundred were killed. In the face of such patent operational failures, how can France argue against Niger's army and civil society drawing the logical conclusion that it's time to change their understanding of the problem and, indeed, change partners, in the fight against terrorism?

CHAPTER 3

NIGER: UNDER THE HEEL OF SERVITUDE AND NEOLIBERALISM

The peoples of West Africa have said no to the servitude of their elites, to neocolonial mechanisms, and to neoliberal dismantling of the State. The neoliberal model, still dominant to this day, has proved far from successful in resolving the pressing problems of the Nigerien people. Take for example the electricity sector. Under Nigerien law, people have a right to electricity, a right which, in principle, guarantees to the rural population access to the services of the modern world.[39] And yet, in 2015, the electric grid serviced just 0.71 percent of rural areas, compared to 54.36 percent of urban areas. Only 9.83 percent of the Nigerien population had access to electricity!

The Electricity Code of Niger was updated in 2003 and 2016. However, neither of these iterations modernized the concession agreement, originally signed in 1993, between the State and NIGELEC, the national electric utility. That has led advocates of privatization to argue that:

> . . . the general policy framework governing the relationship between the State and NIGELEC has remained fixed (as per the statute on Public Enterprises and State Monopolies) since the

enactment of the law that created the utility in 1968, despite a constantly evolving national and international context.[40]

In January 2016, the Energy Sector Regulation Authority (ARSE) was created to break with State control and divvy up the electricity sector "on the basis of multiple actors—public sector and private sector—and in accordance with competition and transparency rules and limits on monopolies."[41] In May 2016, a new Electricity Code was approved. However, this was seen as a backwards step, as it did not provide for "small concessions applicable to Local Rural Electrification Initiatives (ERILs), in parallel with the large rural electrification concessions that will be granted for the State's rural electrification programs."[42] That same year, the Ministry of Energy and Oil published a discussion paper, which underlined the fact that the Code was at cross purposes with the strategy advocated by ARSE inasmuch as it "formalizes NIGELEC's exclusive right to purchase, transport, import, export and distribute electricity."[43] Its authors noted the "breadth and depth of NIGELEC's financial deficit" and flatly rejected

> . . . recurrent operating subsidies to make electricity affordable. The best solution, naturally, is either no subsidies or, in the absence of anything better, the principle of investment subsidies to reduce the costs that rural electrification licensees must bear, with the obligation to integrate such subsidies into the fees schedule for energy services in rural areas.[44]

In other words, private actors would receive government subsidies provided they increase peasant users' electricity bills. This, obviously, would reduce rather than broaden the population's access to electricity. The neoliberal rationale is clearer than water: "the adaptation of governance tools in the electricity sector to the specific requirements of rural electrification is an absolute necessity, given that the State can neither do nor fund everything by itself."[45] According to the precepts of neoliberalism, it's intolerable that "the commercial risk should lie with the State and that the latter should also be responsible for investments." It's an embarrassment that the state subsidizes electricity rates by "setting political prices." Worst of all, "the management framework governing these categories of State-public utilities contracts is utterly bereft of any rationale in terms of economic efficiency."[46] Conclusion: not only is "the role of local communities and non-state actors (i.e., NGOs and civil society) in the electricity sector" excluded, a warm welcome should be extended to foreign governance experts . . .

The neoliberal vision poses the terms of the problem in a biased manner. Neoliberal policy purports to provide access to electricity while simultaneously promoting price liberalization and competition, which should supposedly lower prices when, in reality, there's no guarantee of that happening. When it comes to public sector enterprises, deficits are seen as a crime and scandal, from a business perspective. And yet, what is really at stake is a human right in the broad sense! Must everything be sacrificed on the altar of supply and demand? According to the proponents of privatization, NIGELEC "is falling short in addressing its urban electrification problems and in managing the national electricity grid. Consequently, it would not be appropriate to entrust it with the task of rural electrification."[47]

The privatization model of the 1990s is still extant. In effect, after having rebranded certain measures as "customs modernization reforms," a 2016 IMF report described how "the transfer of customs sub-warehouses management to the private sector was initiated. This process began with the transfer of the customs sub-warehouses managed by the Right Bank Niamey Customs Office to the French transnational Bolloré." Disguising privatization under the misleading rubric of "anti-fraud" measures, the Bolloré Group, a French industrial conglomerate, obtained, in addition to the Directorate-General of Customs, the concession for managing the customs sub-warehouses at the Dosso dry port. The Bolloré Group very succinctly describes its activities as follows:

> Thanks to its strategy of diversification based on innovation and international expansion, the Bolloré Group now occupies solid positions in three sectors: transportation and logistics, communications and electricity storage solutions. With over seventy-nine thousand employees in 130 countries, the Bolloré Group generated sales of nearly €24 billion in 2020.[48]

Bolloré is a multinational heavyweight in the African continent with powerful friends who facilitate its business activities. Thus, in 2015, Bolloré signed concession agreements with the prime ministers of Niger and Benin on the construction and operation of a railroad that would connect Niamey, Niger's capital, with Cotonou, Benin's economic capital. This line was to be managed by Benirail, a new enterprise, whose shares would be allocated as follows: 40 percent for Bolloré, 10 percent for Niger, 10 percent for Benin and 40 percent for private investors from the two countries.

The plan was to construct this railroad by refurbishing part of the old colonial era railroad in Benin. What better symbol could there be of the continuity between the colonialism of yesteryear and that of today? Perhaps Bolloré cherishes dreams of grandeur, of a return to the old days of colonialism. Alas, dreams are sometimes interrupted by a rude awakening. In effect, in 2017, the courts in Benin rejected Bolloré's attempt to take over the part of the railway project that traversed Benin (i.e., the section connecting Cotonou with Niger). This ruling was in response to a suit brought by an entrepreneur named Samuel Dossou, a national of Benin and president of the Petrolin Group. In effect, Dossou alleged that Bolloré had stolen the Benin to Niger railway construction project from Petrolin, which had legal title to the contract, following a successful tender in 2010.

The Petrolin Group had, in fact, asked Bolloré for its assistance as a technical partner, but—according to France 24 journalist Emanuelle Sodji—the conflict arose after Nigerien president Issoufou took office. In effect, the new president, who had:

> . . . no interest in further dealings with Petrolin, asked Bolloré to take over the project. Thomas Boni Yayi, who was then president of Benin, acquiesced and the two governments bet on Bolloré. The Supreme Court of Benin's ruling was very consequential for the Bolloré Group, as the latter had already commenced major construction works in the two countries. In Niger, it had constructed the stretch between Niamey and Dossou, i.e., nearly one hundred kilometers of a railroad in the desert. This is how

the French dream of handling the flow of commodities, especially minerals like Nigerien uranium, from the desert to the ocean, crashed into a wall.[49]

What were President Issoufou's real intentions? Was he intent on modernizing Niger or on helping his Bolloré Group friends in business? On the occasion of the railroad's inauguration, he made the following speech: "Niger is the only country in West Africa, which, until today, did not have a single meter of railroad track." A budget of €142 million . . . and not a single train runs in the country![50] Were it not for the February 2010 coup against President Mamadou Tandja, the project would have known another fate. Under his presidency, the China National Petroleum Corporation began pumping oil in the south eastern part of the country and the China National Nuclear Corporation (CNNC) was granted a concession to mine the Azelik uranium field. France was not pleased with the Nigerien government's cultivation of new partnerships. French Minister of Industry Arnaud Montebourg admitted that the objective of the Bolloré proposal was to block Chinese influence: "The Chinese were prepared to fund this project. So I resolved to find funding. Bolloré told me, 'We will invest two billion and finance the whole project.' For us, this was very advantageous as it didn't require any state funding."[51] In reality, Bolloré had its own plans in mind, namely to operate the magnesium mine in Tambao. In effect, what characterizes this French multinational is its gigantic appetite and equally gigantic arrogance, as attested to, by the way, in its decision to sue Benin and Niger for three billion dollars in damages, following the court ruling in Benin.

Then there's the matter of the 2017–2021 Development Plan (PDES), which was approved by the Issoufou government. This document was not elaborated in accordance with the needs of the Nigerien people but rather, as the following statement indicates, it followed IMF directives: "The PDES is in keeping with international agendas and the Government's 2016–2019 Economic Orientations Paper, which served as the basis for the Economic and Financial Program concluded with the IMF."[52] Perhaps the ex-Areva employee Mr. Issoufou wished to legitimize his rule "by reviving the practice of economic planning, a function of the State that had atrophied during the preceding three decades." In effect, the Constitution of November 25, 2010 contains provisions enabling the renewal of the country's institutions and the launching of a national decentralization policy. As a result of the latter, seven of Niger's regions have approved their own Regional Development Plans.

The previous PDES of 2012–2015 had, in fact, made *"real progress."* Of course, while it was not possible to totally destroy the legacy of the Tandja government, leaving it to the IMF to plan the development of a country like Niger was too great a temptation. What would be the point of achieving a 7 percent growth rate if, at the same time, limits were imposed on the public spending needed to improve living conditions for Nigeriens? What's the point of a development plan if it merely imitates a foreign model doomed to failure? Well, we can judge the development plan based on one of its principal objectives: reduction of the extreme poverty rate from 39.8 percent to 31 percent by 2021. As it happens, not only was this target not achieved by 2021, but the extreme poverty rate actually increased to 41.8 percent.[53]

CHAPTER 4

RAW MATERIALS: THE STORY BEHIND THE STORY

Behind the political spin and narratives is the real story that people need to know, the one revealed by the struggle to control raw materials. This is a story of low blows, agreements signed under the duress of Mafia-like practices, threats, court rulings, repression, and assassinations where the winners are those who are reddest in claw and tooth . . . while the people are left voiceless on the sidelines.

Like many countries in the Global South, in Niger most economic activities take place in the informal economy, which, according to estimates, accounts for over 60 percent of its GDP. According to figures from 2016, the relative weight of the different sectors of Niger's economy were as follows: the primary sector accounted for 38.8 percent of GDP; the tertiary sector, 44.2 percent; and the secondary sector accounted for the remaining 17 percent. Approximately 48 percent of the secondary sector was made up of extractive activities, which in turn consisted mostly of extractive activities (10 percent of the GDP) versus industrial processing activities (7 percent).[54]

What does this economic structure mean for the Nigerien people? First of all, not only does the secondary sector mostly employ unskilled workers exposed to occupational hazards such as industrial accidents and contamination by toxic substances, but, worse still, these jobs will disappear upon depletion of what are, after all, finite mining resources. Mining companies rule wherever they operate and once they close a mine the local community in question becomes a ghost town. Is this the kind of progress and development that young Nigeriens deserve?

With respect to the states of the Sahara-Sahel region, the Congolese historian Elikia M'Bokolo explains that "national unity, the main economic sectors, and political structures" are characterized by

> a very marked fragility. Prior to the colonial period, this area was a major site of contacts between Mediterranean Africa and Tropical Africa. The numerous trans-Saharan trade routes not only enabled major trade flows between the two shores of the Sahara, but they also facilitated constant migratory flows. As a result, the region's modern states are characterized by greater ethnic diversity than elsewhere in Africa (. . .). It wasn't until the mid-1950s that France transformed these territories into potential states. However, these territories lacked a sufficiently solid economic base. Export crops, mainly cotton and peanuts, were not introduced until late in the colonial period and only generated minor trade flows with France. [In Niger], the drought of 1969–1973 struck the country with full force and proved fatal for the regime of Diori Hamani, which was deposed by a military coup in April 1974.[55]

In M'Bokolo's view, "the most worrisome problem remains the chronic food shortages." However, he also highlights an unresolved mystery: despite the spectacular rise in revenues that accompanied the initial years of uranium mining in the country, which rose from 9 percent of export earnings in 1971 to 70 percent in 1978, Niger remains ranked among the countries with the lowest human development indicators.[56] Why did the *uranium boom* fail to benefit Niger?

In the 1970s, Niger became a uranium-producing country under the control and supervision of the French multinational Areva, which monopolized Niger's uranium exports. This resulted in a stagnant and poorly diversified economy. The Nigerien researcher Hamadou D. Youssoufou has collated relevant data points that help us to make sense of the puzzle. Thus, although uranium mined at the Cominak and Sominak mines represented between 75 percent and 90 percent of national income,

> . . . until 2006, tax income from mining was modest, accounting for about 5 to 6 percent of the State's budget resources, or about 1 percent of the GDP. Moreover, this was the case even though uranium exports represented approximately 63 percent of total exports . . . [57]

The bottom line: the mining sector contributed to Niger's economic growth in "a marginal manner, accounting for about 0.3 percent per year between 1990 and 2010."[58] Youssoufou hits the nail on the head in his analysis of how Areva's monopolization of uranium mining was an impediment to the country's development. He concluded that mining in Niger is unconnected with the national economy, functioning instead as an *enclave economy*.

Moreover, uranium was the underlying cause of the coup that overthrew Nigerien president Diori. Youssoufou observes that Diori "was intent on demanding higher yellow cake revenues in a context where the oil crisis resulted in favorable changes in terms of the energy market."[59] The result? On April 14, 1974, four days before scheduled uranium price negotiations, Diori was deposed by a coup.

President Mamadou Tandja (1999–2010) experienced a similar fate. In effect, his mandate was cut short because of his efforts to assert Niger's sovereignty. For example, in 2006, his government passed a new Mining Act that brought an end to France's uranium monopoly. Somina—a consortium between the Government of Niger and the China National Nuclear Corporation—became Areva's primary competitor. In July 2007, tensions with France culminated in the expulsion of Dominique Pin, Areva's director in Niger. This came a month after the expulsion of Areva-Niger's head of security, the ex-Colonel Gilles de Namur. The proximate cause of these tensions was the Tandja administration's accusation that France was financing Tuareg rebels.[60] The Government of Niger took further action when it announced its intention to transfer Areva's mining concessions to its rivals. By exposing France's double dealing, the Tandja government put itself in a strong negotiating position. It took advantage of this strong position to demand a 50 percent increase in the price of the uranium mined from the Cominak and Somair mines over the next two years, and to approve the Imarouren mining project, a new source of income that would benefit the State. Given that 80 percent of France's electricity production comes from uranium imported from Niger, it's reasonable to conclude that even after these changes to existing agreements France would still come out as a winner. After all, the reason for France's presence in Niger is the necessity to dispose of a strategic raw material on highly favorable terms. According to Areva, the Imarouren mining project would require an estimated investment of €1 billion to mine about five thousand tons per year. The Tandja government was also guilty of diversifying its mining partners and developing close relations with leaders like Qadafi and with a country like Venezuela, with which it signed an energy cooperation agreement on September 27, 2009.

In February 2017, the "uraniumgate" scandal erupted when the magazine *Le Courrier* published a document on a $320 million uranium transaction in late 2011. Said document outlined a kickback scheme that proceeded as follows: Areva sold a quantity of uranium, worth $320 million, to Energo Alyans, a Russian shell company, for $220 million, which then resold this uranium for $302.2 million to Optima Energy Offshore, a Swiss company (whose CEO was Jean-Claude Meyer), thereby earning a profit of $82 million! The circle was closed when the government in Niamey, acting through the Niger National Mine Assets Corporation (*Société du patrimoine des mines du Niger*—SOPAMIN), purchased the uranium for $319.8 million. In the end, SOPAMIN pocketed $850,000 while Areva-Niger lost $101 million.[61]

Under questioning during a parliamentary investigation, Hassoumi Massaoudou, then Niger's Minister of Finance, stated that he received a phone call from Areva Board Member Sébastien de Montessus who "only wanted to use SOPAMIN as a nominal buyer. He said that Niger would make money in this operation." According to the testimony of his French collaborators, in March 2012, a $2.6 million kickback was deposited in President

Mahamadou Issoufou's account in Dubai. The Nigerien parliament's report on the investigation found the state innocent in this affair, with Areva being the sole guilty party. The opposition parties, however, denounced this investigation, calling it bungled and lacking in integrity, as the two barristers who had initiated it were subsequently excluded from its proceedings.

Massaoudou, who remained Issoufou's right-hand man, was named the Minister of State to the Presidency and later became Foreign Minister under the Bazoum administration. After the coup in July 2023, thanks to the latter cabinet post, he was able to maintain contact with European governments, including Germany's and Denmark's, and subsequently announce that the latter supported without reservation a military intervention against Niger to return Bazoum to power. Such fulsome enthusiasm for war is, shall we say, surprising. An inquiring (and suspicious) mind might wonder if this might be a way to avoid the reopening of judicial proceedings against the former foreign minister.

Until recently, Niger was dependent on oil imports. In 1975, in a context of fast-rising primary commodity prices, the neighboring countries of Benin and Nigeria created national oil companies to exercise a monopoly on the supply side. Niger followed suit by creating the Nigerien Petroleum Products Corporation (*Société nigérienne des produits pétroliers*—SONIDEP), a state-owned enterprise to secure the country's oil supply. The objective was to change the rules then in force, which benefited private oil distribution companies.[62] In the 1990s, Niamey also became intent on diversifying its energy sources. This was accomplished by substituting dependence on oil imports from Nigeria, which presented certain problems, with a turn towards the international market via the Burkina Faso/Togo route, as well as via shipments from the port of Cotonou, in Benin, to Parakou on Niger's southern border.

In 1994, the State decided, in the interests of Niger's energy security, to increase the country's strategic oil reserve from a capacity of forty-eight days to seventy-two days by investing 11 billion CFA francs in an expansion project. This investment was criticized as "disproportionate" by foreign analysts favorable to privatization. In the words of a 1995 report published by the American transnational auditing firm Ernst & Young: "Without an increase in sales volumes, SOPAMIN will be unable to bear the additional costs incurred by the Niamey strategic reserve (i.e., the depreciation, maintenance, and operating costs)."[63] Although it's true that the country's leaders have used SOPAMIN to resolve the State's financial difficulties . . . and to enrich their families, is one to believe that Ernst & Young is disinterested in its concerns about the Nigerien State's financial health? When the unipolar capitalist world was at its zenith in the 1990s, Ernst & Young was crystal clear in its worldview, as attests the title of a book it published in 1994: *Privatization: Investing in State-Owned Enterprises around the World*.

In summary, for Ernst & Young, "privatization is not only an economic buzzword. It's synonymous with investment opportunities with unlimited upside potential." Nor is it a coincidence that at the very moment that the government was preparing to privatize SONIDEP, based on a plan designed by the IMF and the World Bank, petroleum multinationals Exxon and Elf were undertaking new exploration activities in eastern Niger. After the decline in world uranium prices, the share of the Nigerien state's fiscal revenues from the hydrocarbons sector was about 20 percent per year. To the present day, state subsidies for the oil sector in Nigeria have encouraged illegal gasoline imports from Niger's southern neighbor, which has cost SONIDEP considerable losses in income.

Researcher Vincent Caupin wonders whether, "by authorizing duty-free sales, the State is breaking the law and cutting its own tax revenues. In this context, it's legitimate to wonder what motivates the authorities." Caupin then describes how political leaders prefer the recourse to clientelism with their followers and relations to "consolidate their authority." Labazé, for his part, writes that "the allocation of profits from these commercial operations between traders, influential civil servants, and members of the security services is governed by a very precise mechanism."[64]

In 2010, SONIDEP was in the headlines and at the center of the country's political intrigues. As Moussa Naganou, the editor of several private media outlets, explains:

> . . . it was on the basis of a mysterious SONIDEP account that president Tandja Mamadou was indicted following a sham lifting of immunity by the State Tribunal. Following this ruling, the military regime of Salou Djibo was able to formally imprison Tandja Mamadou by citing a folder that contained four billion of our francs, withdrawn from SONIDEP. After February 18, 2010, the date of the coup, Tandja was illegally detained under police custody in Villa Verte. For eleven months, until January 16, 2011, this detention was automatically extended, in contravention of a ruling from the ECOWAS Court of Justice which ordered his release. It was only when SONIDEP divulged a tiny fraction of its secrets, that he was transferred to the Kollo penal camp, which is where the

old man was confined from January 16 to May 10, 2011.[65]

Under the heel of neocolonial interests and a corrupt leadership class, the Nigerien people were not in a position to benefit from the country's extraordinary mineral resources. Astonishingly, this oil-producing country is plagued by gasoline shortages! The year before the nationalist coup of July 26, 2023, Nigerien civil society protested against a 24 percent increase in the price of diesel. As representative Omar Tchiana put it in the National Assembly:

> . . . Nigeriens rightly wonder why the government's administration of such a national resource is captained by a gang of cronies who share out contracts, government tenders, the transportation and pipeline markets, and much more to the disgust of the rest of the population.[66]

Representative Tchiana then suggested the following solution to the Oil Minister:

> . . . he must dismantle this clique of five persons who have usurped Nigeriens' oil and who only distribute gasoline to their chums' gas stations, concessions to their members, and travel vouchers to their cronies.[67]

Tchiana further recalled how the construction of the Soraz national refinery in 2008, thanks to Chinese capital, had been the object of both "rejection by western oil companies and scathing criticism by the opposition of that time"; and that its operation "which, today, is our pride and joy, is subject to all kinds of insinuations due to the lack of transparency in its management."[68]

The Nigerien transition government, along with the social movements which are its base of support, took the irrevocable decision to declare French ambassador Sylvain Itté persona non grata. According to all appearances, President Macron is, against every rule in diplomacy, utilizing this affair to inflame public opinion rather than to call for cooler heads to prevail. Notwithstanding the issuance of a warrant for his arrest and an expulsion order by the Nigerien legal authorities, Itté went into hiding in the French embassy, arguing that the only authority he recognized was ex-president Bazoum. What type of ambassador would decide to remain in a country as an "unauthorized alien"? What mission might he be tasked with in a country that does not desire his presence, other than to sow division and hatred among Nigeriens and call for a military invasion? Particular utterances he has made in recent years are remembered by Nigeriens as the very embodiment of colonial arrogance. For example, Itté once infamously said that Nigeriens "should stop drinking water because water is European."[69]

Did the privatization of the Niger National Water Assets Corporation (*Société de Patrimoine des Eaux du Niger*—SPEN), now owned by the French multinational Veolia, give Itté the right to mock the Nigerien people in this way?[70]

As it happens, there've been proposals to construct the Kandadji dam on the Niger River—Africa's third longest after the Nile and the Congo rivers and whose source is in Guinea—on a location close to the border with Mali. Despite its strategic character for Niger, this water resources megaproject has not advanced an inch since the 1970s. And yet, this project would enable Niger

to double its electricity generation and reduce its dependency on Nigeria. By irrigating nearly forty-five thousand
hectares, the Kandadji Dam would be comparable in scale
to the Aswan Dam, which was constructed in the 1960s,
in the Egypt of Gamal Abdul Nasser, with the Soviet
Union providing about a third of the financing. In Niger
as well, the project included Russian participation when
it was approved in 2009. However, after the coup against
president Tandja, work on the project was suspended. In
2019, the China Gezhouba Group Company (CGGC)
took over the construction works, which are scheduled for
completion in 2025.

Fortunately, prospects are changing in Niger, one
of the poorest countries in the world. The discovery of
a major oil field in Kafra, in northern Niger, near the
Algerian border, could signify much-coveted national
energy independence. In effect, Niger's dependence on oil
imports could be transformed into exports of surplus production to neighboring countries. In 2018, the company
responsible for oil exploration was SIPEX, an international subsidiary of the Algerian company Sonatrech.
As it happens, Algeria has an interest in connecting its
pipelines from northern Niger to Gaya, in south eastern
part of the country, on the border with Benin, which
would create the longest pipeline in Africa. The increase
in Nigerien oil production would be from 20,000 barrels
per day (BPD) to as much as 110,000 BPD, of which
90,000 BPD would be exported by pipeline to Sémé, a
port city in Benin.

Oil would become a primary source of income for
the Nigerien state, generating over $4 billion per year,
i.e., a quarter of the GDP and 50 percent of its fiscal revenues. The nearly two-thousand-kilometer-long pipeline,
which was under construction with the participation of

contractors from WAPCO, a subsidiary of the Chinese company CNPC, had an estimated completion date of October or November 2023, at the time of the nationalist coup. Close to 20,000 BPD would have served to satisfy domestic consumption, which in recent years has been around 7,000 BPD, while 90,000 BPD would have been exported. Nigeria, long a major world oil producer, would therefore see its neighbor become a minor supplier to the world market. That said, given that Nigeria produces nearly 2 million BPD,[71] Niger was not about to become a serious rival. On the other hand, given their complementary character, Niger's relations with Benin were bound to strengthen. However, these plans to export Nigerien oil on the world market ran into the proverbial immovable object, namely the closing of the border with Benin and the tight blockade imposed by ECOWAS sanctions in response to the coup against Mohamed Bazoum. These measures against Niger compromised the commissioning of the crude oil export pipeline, which was officially scheduled for early 2024.

The proposed dam and oil pipeline are not the only twenty-first century megaprojects liable to put Niger on the map in Africa in capital letters. For several years, there have been two competing natural gas pipeline projects. Neither of these projects, which would follow different routes, has yet been built. However, with the war in Ukraine, an energy security crisis emerged which has turned them into urgent projects. In effect, they would offer an alternative non-Russian source of natural gas. The first and more viable gas pipeline project would connect Nigeria with Algeria, from whence gas would be distributed to various ports on the other side of the Mediterranean.

The firm support that Algeria gave Niger during the post-coup crisis is explained by its determination to complete the trans-Saharan Nigal gas pipeline project. The aforementioned Algerian state-owned enterprise Sonatrech would very likely participate in this project, which would strengthen its position as a natural gas exporter in world markets. In this regard, it's also important to remember that Spain's unexpected support for Morocco on the Saharawi issue in 2022 led to a diplomatic crisis with Algeria. Moreover, as a consequence of the war in Ukraine, natural gas prices have skyrocketed. These developments led Sonatrech to raise its gas prices for the Spanish market and to seek a renegotiation of the existing terms of its agreement with Spain to ensure that gas transits through the Medgaz pipeline, which connects Spain with the natural gas fields in Algeria. In the end, Spain, which, until recently, sourced half of its natural gas imports from Algeria, was obliged to diversify its partners, with the United States as the primary beneficiary.

The Nigal gas pipeline project has yet to go forward for different reasons. As a result, other actors have forged ahead in favor of another project: the African-Atlantic gas pipeline,[72] an underwater pipeline that would begin in Nigeria and run along the coastal countries of West Africa up to Morocco. On June 10, 2018, this initiative was approved under a cooperation agreement signed by Mohammadu Buharu, then Nigeria's president, and the Kingdom of Morocco. This 5,660-kilometer pipeline would be an extension of an existing pipeline from Nigeria to Ghana which transits Benin and Togo. If, instead of the Nigal pipeline, this project went ahead, then Niger and Algeria would be the losers. Nigeria, on the other hand, would be a winner regardless of which of the two projects is completed.

The patriotic military junta of the CNSP could not have anticipated that the response to Bazoum's removal from power would be so hostile and intransigent. That said, the CNSP had no doubts about who benefits from the country's exports of primary commodities and it's not the people. No, it is a corrupt and compromised elite in the service of foreign powers who benefit. Above all, if Bazoum had remained in power, the anti-terrorist struggle would still be sabotaged from within, moves towards new partnerships would have been prevented and the status quo maintained. As it happens, the timing of the nationalist military coup in Niger was propitious. The Islamist attack in Anzourou, which killed twelve persons on July 12, 2023, was the straw that broke the camel's back. President Bazoum's close military cooperation with France and the cooling of relations with Mali were exposed as ineffective and dangerous, as attested, notably, the absence of a security policy for the Tillabéri region, located on the strategic border area with Mali and Burkina Faso.

Bazoum made the fatal error of neglecting relations with neighboring countries and delegating the "anti-terrorist struggle" to actors who calmly made their decisions in French military bases or in Paris. The CNSP's request for assistance from Russia, in the form of military advisors or the Wagner mercenary group, was incompatible with the existing security agreements and protocols between France and Niger. Consequently, one of the CNSP's first measures was to cancel them. That decision represented a setback for imperialism, especially since it coincided with the Russia-Africa Summit Meeting and came just a month before the BRICS 2023 meeting. There was no shortage at that time of voices from France and other NATO countries pushing Russiaphobic propaganda to delegitimize Russia's influence in Africa by framing it in the worst possible ways. A new McCarthy-style witch hunt is under way. Anything or anyone with the slightest connection with Russia is suspect. Be that as it may, the real question is: How could things possibly go worse for the countries of the Sahel? The fact that a country like the Central African Republic requires Russian military advisors simply shows that when it comes to defending a country's sovereignty it's only pragmatic considerations that matter. As far as assistance is concerned, it's effectiveness that counts, not flowery speeches.

CHAPTER 5

RUSSIA BEHIND THE SCENES: MYTHS AND REALITIES

Coincidentally, the coup in Niamey occurred at the same time as the Russia-Africa Summit, where the pro-Russian tone of Captain Ibrahim Traoré did not go unremarked. That was enough for the Western-dominated media to sound the alarm. Moreover, just as Mali welcomed the Wagner Private Military Company after the French military was expelled, it now seemed that Niger might follow the same path. Not only that, but, simplifying their reasoning in the extreme, certain influential voices directly blamed Moscow for the coup. "Russia is behind the demonstration against the French embassy in Niamey." Or so said General Dominique Trinquand, the former head of the French military mission at the UN, in an interview with the private broadcaster TF1, where the general was introduced as a simple "expert." The French news channel BFM likewise interviewed the spokesperson for the general staff of the French army. Evidently, when it comes to such sensitive issues, propaganda from the army is preferable to the keen eyes of independent analysts. After all, didn't former French Interior Minister Manuel Valls once say—in a context marked by terrorism—that "explaining the causes [of terrorist acts] is equivalent to justifying them."

In reality, a coalition of NGOs known as the M62 social movement played a fundamental role in how the military rebellion unfolded by organizing multiple opposition demonstrations against Bazoum and in support of the CNSP. This movement, whose name is a reference to the sixty-second anniversary of independence, pushed the CNSP to adopt measures based on a national liberation and Pan-African perspective.

Historically, over the decades, the pro-sovereignty wing of the Nigerien army had tried, without success, to change the course of events in favor of fairer negotiations over the terms of trade for primary commodities. This interest in politics on the part of certain senior African military officers stems from their awareness that economic sovereignty is a logical extension of national sovereignty, which it is their mission to defend, regardless of the Eurocentric point of view, which denounces any intrusion into politics by the military. Thus, provided that the problem of corruption among senior military officers is overcome—a problem fostered by neocolonialism—an army in the Global South can impose a new correlation of forces with greater success than political leaders accustomed to corruption. The army is a key institution in "protonations," a term coined by Jean Ziegler, to describe African nations characterized by an unfinished process of independence:

> The protonation is the product of a particular conjuncture in the evolution of imperialism. It is, in effect, engendered by the reorientation, reconfiguration and rebalancing of the imperialist system that emerged after the Second World War. Imperialism decided to affect a formal transfer of power to indige-

nous social classes, which it itself had created and continues to dominate through symbolic violence. In summary, contemporary French-speaking black Africa mainly consists of either protonations or structures of repression. No nation is born without a lengthy war and, consequently, without breaking with the capitalist mode of production, foreign capital and the ties of submission with its military, political, and ideological agent: the metropolitan (colonial) State.

In a word, this long war is not won with speeches at the UN. The military escalation between NATO and Russia may have legitimized the role of the armed forces in African countries, which felt relegated to the margins of the world geopolitical chess board. That, however, does not mean that they are in a position to play this role freely without interference. Consequently, it's vital that they carefully determine who their partners should be. Contrary to Western propaganda, with the exception of NATO member countries, only a minority of the world's governments are favorable to sanctions against Russia. The fact that African countries were unanimous in voting against the sanctions against Russia is not unimportant. A report published in the US by the Atlantic Council makes the following observations in relation to Africa and the war in Ukraine:

> Africa emerged as a major player in this conflict on March 3, 2022, when seventeen African states abstained from voting on the United Nations General Assembly resolution condemning the Russian invasion of

Ukraine. The number of abstaining countries was surprising, as well as which specific
nations abstained; some, like Morocco and
Senegal, are known for their proximity to the
Western camp. (. . .) Finally, some nations
wished to remain non-aligned with either of
the belligerents, so as not to threaten commercial relationships, or simply remain neutral
towards a war that did not concern them.[73]

African governments sent a clear message by opting
unanimously to maintain trade relations with Russia.
While cooperation and closer relations between Russia
and Africa, on every level, is something the West eyes with
fear, the peoples of Africa are supportive of relations they
perceive as evidence that their governments are pursuing
sovereign and independent policies.

The volume of trade between Russia and Africa doubled
between 2015 and 2023 and is now valued at $20 billion per
year. Above all, Russia has increased its economic cooperation through major projects such as the negotiation of
nuclear energy agreements between Rosatom, a Russian
state-owned enterprise, and at least sixteen African countries. Another major project is the $7 billion Russian indus-
trial park in Egypt's Suez Canal Zone.

The relations between Africa and Russia left an
enduring mark when the African peoples were engaged
in their anti-colonial struggles. As historian Elikia
M'Bokolo observes "between 1954 and 1972, the Soviet
Union carried out, alone or in collaboration with other
socialist states, nearly 350 projects, mainly in seven
countries: Algeria, Ethiopia, Ghana, Guinea, Mali, and
Sudan."[74] In an interview with the author, the Guinean
trade unionist Mamadou Mansaré stated that Soviet assis-

tance was essential for the liberation movements based in Algeria, then known as "the Mecca of revolutionaries." As Mansaré explains:

> I worked for the Kindia Bauxite Company (*Société des bauxites de Kindia*—SBK), an enterprise created with the express purpose of paying the Russians for the arms that the USSR and other countries of the Soviet Bloc sent us, arms which we then distributed to different national liberation movements. We shipped our first contribution to the FLN [National Liberation Front] in Algeria. The arms that arrived in Guinea were then sent to Bamako, from whence they were transported across the desert before their final delivery to Boumédienne.[75]

Guinea was the first African country to reject France's neocolonial plans. Its solidarity with fraternal liberation movements in Algeria, South Africa, Mozambique, Angola, Zambia, Zimbabwe, or Guinea-Bissau was authentic and based on the ideal of Pan-African liberation. The Soviet Union also played a crucial, if not totally disinterested, role:

> All of these countries received assistance from the Guinean government through bauxite mining companies. We used to ship our bauxite on Russian ships to Ukraine where a plant was built in order to process our bauxite. The Nikolaev plant was the foundation for what became today's Russal Group. Today, it's a large mining conglomerate, but during

the Soviet empire Nikolaev was a state-owned enterprise. The Nikolaev plant was built to transform bauxite into aluminum and to repay the debt owed the Soviet Bloc for the arms, teachers, and doctors they sent us, as well as to fund the infrastructure we were building.[76]

Russia can hardly be blamed for seeking to reactivate its influence in Africa by invoking the history of its relations with countries during the era of decolonization. Likewise, Europeans should be honest enough to acknowledge the Red Army's contribution in the fight against fascism. Moreover, Europeans should prove through their actions that they no longer have a colonial mentality. They can do this by supporting the present-day struggles of the peoples of Africa and Latin America. In contrast with Europeans, whose recent history has either been erased or "creatively curated,"* when Africans consider their past or present, they know how to distinguish between words and actions.

Why didn't the countries of the Third World emulate the Industrial Revolution, which, by the end of the nineteenth century, had spread from England to faraway Russia and Japan? The answer, as the Belgian historian Paul Bairoch explains, is that:

> . . . during the period when the Industrial Revolution should have been spontaneously spreading to most areas of the Third World, the

---

*   [Author's note as of August 2024] Especially during and after the Cold War, when the role of the Soviet Union in the decisive fight against German Nazism was relegated to oblivion by demonizing Russia, passing sanctions against it and censoring the media financed by that state.

great majority of those territories had already fallen under colonial domination, some more directly, others less so. This colonial domination likely largely explains the Industrial Revolution's failure to spread further in the course of the nineteenth century.[77]

The Industrial Revolution and the progress that it brought failed to spread because

> . . . at that the time the structure and substantive content of progress had already changed, which thereby rendered it not only much less accessible and difficult to transfer (if only due to the greater technical complexity thereof), but also reduced the likelihood that any embryonic development would automatically engender a self-perpetuating growth process.[78]

Therefore, once the countries of Africa became independent, it was imperative to put a development strategy on the agenda that would enable technology transfer and technical training to lay the foundations for a break with the preceding era. In fact, this issue was foreseen by the former colonial power. However, in a continent immense with mineral resources, the new nations of Africa were forced to maintain the status quo, which favored France at the expense of their own populations.

Yash Tandon, a former presidential advisor to the government of Uganda, has written a clear and compelling account of the neocolonial blackmail methods used by the West to maintain its dominance of the African continent. The story he tells should serve as a permanent reminder of how a certain ideological discourse minimizes the

West's responsibility for today's situation of dependence. Tandon tried to change Uganda's economic structure to achieve true autonomy, but those efforts came to an end when a coup installed dictator Idi Amin's bloody reign from 1971 to 1979.

After long experience working with marginalized and impoverished peasant communities in Zimbabwe and Tanzania, Professor Tandon founded the Southern and Eastern Africa Trade Information and Negotiations Institute (CEATINI) with the objective of helping African countries to negotiate more effectively with neocolonial institutions. In his book *Trade is War: The West's War against the World*,[79] Tandon describes how the World Trade Organization (WTO) set aside the issues that the United Nations Conference on Trade and Development (UNCTAD) used to address, replacing them with new ones such as intellectual property, telecommunications, genetically modified organisms, etc. Twenty-three years of working with peasants in rural areas taught him that:

> … the majority of traditional African medicines come from trees, i.e. from their bark, shrubs and roots. One used to see representatives from pharmaceutical companies dressed in white lab coats come and take samples from crops and tree bark, as well as human blood, sputum and saliva samples. This knowledge taken from Africa would then be converted into patented medicines, which they sell back to us, charging exorbitant prices![80]

Some will say that Western imperialism only did what any business would do. Here's Tandon's response:

. . . private property is foundational to the capitalist system. However, intellectual property only became part of the global system in the last fifty years, more or less. Formerly, each country was able to industrialize by copying other countries' technology. The United States did this with England, and later Europe, including Switzerland and others, did likewise. Everyone copied the know-how and then later patented it. Today, Switzerland is one of the largest manufacturers of pharmaceuticals based on knowledge stolen and patented by Swiss businesses. First they steal the knowledge, and then they monopolize it! Intellectual property was integrated into the global system in the last fifty years. Formerly, each country could industrialize by copying the technology of others. (. . .) China was able to industrialize because it obtained free technological know-how from the Soviet Union in the 1950s. The Soviet Union, which did not have a patents system, also provided know-how to India. This is why the first automobiles manufactured there were based on Soviet models.[81]

What then, is the crux of the question? The Russia of today is not the Russia of yesteryear. That said, Vladimir Putin is seen by the United States as a strategic enemy to be defeated and that is leading to a new Cold War. That, in turn, leaves the countries of the Global South with two possibilities: they can either submit, or instead "create two, three, or many Vietnams" and thereby defeat, temporarily or permanently, the empire's strategies.

In recent years, Russia has become the African continent's main arms supplier. Researcher Agnès Verdebout describes the policy followed since Putin became president of the Russian Federation:

> In 2006, the Kremlin forgave a debt owed by Algeria, worth an estimated $4.7 billion, in exchange for the signing of a $7.5 billion contract for fighter jets, air defense missiles, and tanks. The same model was applied with Libya in 2008, where debts totaling $4.6 billion were canceled and a cooperation agreement valued at an estimated $10 billion was signed (which included $4 billion worth of arms contracts). [82]

According to a report by GRIP, a Belgian peace and security think tank, the sanctions against Russia have not had their intended effect:

> Russia is able turn to alternative partners both to obtain the technologies it needs to manufacture its arms systems, as well as to offset financial losses incurred due to sanctions on oil and gas sales to Europe, and thereby support its arms production. [83]

The arms contract between Russia and Algeria has made the latter an object of scrutiny in the US Congress. [84] In its attempts to ruin the Russian economy, the United States is acting in violation of international law. In effect, it has implemented two custom-made mechanisms to enforce sanctions on an extraterritorial basis: the Countering America's Adversaries through Sanctions Act

(CAATSA) and the Foreign Direct Product Rule (FDPR). For the United States, the inclusion of a country on its list of countries representing a national security threat is sufficient reason to prohibit exports to said country of "the majority of technologies and programs utilized in the manufacture of the semiconductors employed in all modern devices, including numerous arms systems."[85] Agnès Verdebout highlights the FDPR's impact on the "Russian military industrial complex" by observing that the semiconductors value chain is "still highly internationalized and interdependent," a fact which "confines to the margins design and manufacturing processes which do not use US origin technologies."[86] Verdebout emphasizes that CAATSA even allows the US to apply sanctions against NATO members, which indeed occurred when Turkey acquired S-400 air-defense missiles from Russia.

In a country like the Central African Republic, the French cure proved, yet again, worse than the disease. In 2013, my colleague Olivier Ndenkop, who is a Cameroonian journalist, described the chaos orchestrated by France as follows:

> Looting, rape, and serial killing are becoming routine activities for these men trained in brutality and massacres! Once the chain of command has been broken and wonderful promises are not kept, nobody is in control of anything. The country is in the same state of ungovernability as Libya was when it was invaded by Jihadis, in the aftermath of the assassination of the Guide Muammar Qadafi by NATO troops, with the France of [former president] Sarkozy and BHL [public intellectual Bernard-Henri Lévy] leading the

way. The situation in the Central African
Republic is strangely reminiscent of what
happened in Abidjan after the overthrow of
Laurent Gbagbo by the pro-Outtara rebels,
with French support. In effect, after the fall of
Côte d'Ivoire's then head of state, elements of
"the New Forces" (the rebellion led by Guil-
laume Soro, current speaker of the National
Assembly) were swindled. These elements had
been promised money and other perks during
the fight against the Gbagbo regime, but these
promises were not kept when Ouattara took
office as President of the Republic. In reprisal,
the "New Forces" sacked the Ivoirian capital,
but not without first torturing and killing a
number of innocent merchants.[87]

The French military operation "Sangaris," which
began in December 2013 and ended in October 2016,
failed to prevent numerous massacres, including the ones
in Bouar, Boali (twice), Bossembelé, Bossemptelé, Baoro
... According to a UN commission of inquiry, in 2013–
2014, the conflict caused between three thousand and six
thousand deaths and displaced a half million persons. The
new Central African authorities have, however, since laid
the groundwork for new and more balanced international
relations through security and defense cooperation with
Russia. The following assessment of the first five years of
Russo-Central African cooperation was made by a minister and special advisor to president Touadéra:

> The results are eloquent and our assessment
> is positive because, five years ago, the Central
> African Republic was considered the most

dangerous place in the world. Today, one can communicate with the Central African Republic and visit it. We avoided a fratricidal war in 2020–2021 (. . .) The war was provoked by General Bozizé, but thanks to the defense agreement between the number one nuclear power in the world, the Russian Federation, and the Central African Republic, we were able to save our democracy with the assistance of the Russian soldiers put at our disposal under the terms of this agreement.[88]

However, not every government is ready to protect its people at the risk of annoying the US Empire. President Bola Tinubu of Nigeria, for instance, has on several occasions threatened a regional military intervention with incalculable consequences. As researcher Ike Okonta suggests, Tinubu would be better advised to attend to his population:

> . . . the most common error is the belief that Nigeria is a rich country. It isn't, although it is potentially rich. Currently, 80 percent of our budget depends on oil revenues. Moreover, our GDP is actually quite low given the country's population of 170 million. Finally, poor use is made of the little money that is at our disposal due to corruption.[89]

In principle, gas and oil revenues should be a source of development. However, while "many oil concessions were granted to persons in the north [of Nigeria], these persons did not invest in their region."

Why this regional failure to invest?

Governance is feudal and revolves around the interests of the emirs. Consequently, their strategy focuses on limiting access to education for the mass of the population, which is accomplished by sending children to very basic Koranic schools. It is this legacy which explains Boko Haram's fortunes.[90]

According to Okonta:

> ... when Boko Haram emerged around the year 2000, some politicians in the north saw an opportunity to put the State in a difficult situation. Unless structural problems are resolved, things will become extremely difficult (...) Since the 1980s and the IMF structural adjustment plan, Nigeria has been deindustrializing. The government has not played its role. It has failed to find a solution to the problem of unemployment.[91]

What would happen if the Government of Nigeria were to decide, free of outside pressure, to set a new course? Without a doubt, it would be its turn to face the threat of military intervention. However, when one has little to lose and much to gain that's a risk worth taking. As for Niger, it has decided to follow the path blazed by Mali and Burkina Faso, by joining forces with them and by opting for a new defense and security partner. Will that break the vicious circle of pillage and impunity? Russia is not behind the scenes, pulling the strings of peoples struggling for their sovereignty. No, Russia is at their side and that allows them to take a breather before waging new battles.

In fact, what really warrants scrutiny is the US' discreet role in the region. There are, in fact, two US military bases in Niger:[92] Air Base 101 near the Niamey airport and Air Base 201. The latter is a drone base and considered "the pentagon's main intelligence base in the Sahel." After the closing of the French base and the expulsion of France's troops, the 1,100 American soldiers in Niger will be walking on a tightrope. Cognizant of this situation, on September 7, the Pentagon ordered the redeployment of its troops in Niamey to northern Niger "for precautionary reasons." The real question, which everyone's asking, is: Which African country will be the next to join the revolution?

CHAPTER 6

PAN-AFRICAN UNITY AGAINST WESTERN TERRORISM

As we've seen, a proper account of current events in Niger requires taking into consideration the recent history of the African continent. Contrary to the claims of a certain propaganda discourse, the demands of the Nigerien people do not arise from anti-French sentiment owing to populism and shoddy after-sales customer service on the part of colonialism. Today's French colonialists claim that China, Russia, and even the United States are just as paternalistic as they are. According to imperialist ideology, the historic defeat of colonialism was merely a problem of poor communication. In reality, not only were the Nigerien people never of any importance to the colonialists, but, on the contrary, they sought to sabotage Niger's initiatives to strengthen its sovereignty and achieve real independence.

French governments have lied, are lying, and will continue to lie to assert their control over cheap African resources. To that end, they've allied with terrorist groups and will continue to do so, as attests their actions in Libya, Syria, and other countries. The problem is that the peoples of the Global South no longer listen to the Western media. The media war has intensified since the NATO countries imposed censorship on the Russian media. The revolutionary governments of Mali, Burkina Faso, and Niger are well aware of the duplicity practiced by Radio France Internationale and France 24. Consequently, they are ill disposed to allow said media to manipulate their populations. Ever since the revelations regarding Operation Mockingbird in the United States, we know that a large number of intelligence agents operate right inside the newsrooms of the major Western media.

To protect its interests, France counts on vassal states that bend to the dictates of Western foreign policy, such as Côte d'Ivoire, Senegal, Nigeria, and Chad. On April 21, 2021, the Chadian opposition denounced an "institutional coup" and a "dynastic transfer of power"[93] when the son of President Idriss Déby Itno, an ally of France, took power upon his father's death. This succession was immediately recognized by Macron, who paid fulsome homage to the new president's late father. What did it matter that Déby Itno had seized power thirty years ago and was detested by the people? The only thing that mattered was the loyal services he rendered to the Western powers as a key partner in the "fight against terrorism" in the Sahel.

Similarly, in Senegal, in the midst of the crisis triggered by the coup in Niger, the regime of Macky Sall jailed Ousmane Sonko, the opposition's principal leader and leading candidate in the upcoming 2024 elections. Sall also suspended internet access to block the flow of information and thwart mass protests while the security forces carried on repressing and killing demonstrators in the streets. In addition, in a move to divert attention, the regime threatened to participate in the ECOWAS military intervention by sending its troops to Niger. Meanwhile, the Western powers and media said nothing in the face of twenty-eight deaths by gunfire, in just four days in June 2023—a toll that would only grow in the following weeks.

The West and its media likewise remained mute regarding reports of torture under Sall's bloody regime.

In September 1957, Frantz Fanon explained in an article in *El Moujahid*, a publication of Algeria's National Liberation Front (FLN), that "the first tactic of colonial countries consists of relying on official collaborators and feudal lords."[94] That observation remains valid in the era of neocolonialism. Although it will be some time before historians clarify today's unfolding events, that does not prevent African peoples from having a keen awareness of the lessons of history. As Teniola Tayo, a researcher with the French Institute for African Studies (IFRA-Nigeria), observes:

> . . . everything happens as if, since the end of the colonial period, there's never been any nation-building in the country (. . .) Every actor defends their own interests because they view the state as incapable of protecting the people of Nigeria.[95]

This type of situation is exactly what that the multinationals of imperialist countries need to manipulate certain sectors of society and destabilize the state. This is how resource rich African countries were riven by secessionist movements supported and organized by the West. This explains the birth of terrorist militias like Boko Haram, which later spread to Cameroon, Chad, and Niger. The French government's support for the secession of Biafra, an eastern province of Nigeria, in the late 1960s, offers a perfect example of how different elements are coordinated in the service of neocolonial crimes.

As the historian Benoît Collombat explains, Biafra's secession was organized with the support of two logistics bases, one in Côte d'Ivoire (in West Africa) and the other in Gabon (in Central Africa). The dispatching of arms and mercenaries, together with the use of "cynical propaganda to manipulate the press and humanitarian groups," was intended to destabilize Nigeria, "a giant English-speaking country perceived as an objective ally of the Soviets in Africa."[96] The Nigeria of that era had rapidly piled up "demerit points," in contrast, for instance, with France's vassal Félix Houphouët-Boigny, the president of Côte d'Ivoire. For example, when, in January 1961, the president of Nigeria expelled the French ambassador to protest France's atomic tests in the Algerian Sahara, the French government's reaction was swift, taking the form of support for the Igbo ethnic group to encourage a secessionist movement in a country then expected to develop into Africa's largest economy. On May 30, 1967, Biafra declared its independence. It was no coincidence that two thirds of Nigeria's oil fields were located in Biafra, where, since 1964, oil production was carried out by SAFRAP (a subsidiary of the ERAP Group, as ELF was then known), as part of the Shell-British Petroleum (BP) consortium.

At the end of the 1970s, after Biafra's failed secession, patriotic military officers nationalized BP's assets in Nigeria and "became the champions of Pan-African cooperation, financing several African liberation movements. The interests of the West and Nigeria repeatedly clashed, but Nigeria always stood its ground."[97] While one may accuse the African governments that are vassals to Western multinationals of many things, naivety is not one of them. Thus, Nigeria's current president, who has betrayed the cause of Niger's liberation, is most certainly not ignorant of African history or of his country's leading role therein. However, just in case, let's remind some of his confused followers of that history:

In October 2007, Umaru Musa Yar'Adua (president of Nigeria, 2007–2010) joined South Africa and Libya in opposing the plans of the United States to deploy Africom, which could potentially serve as an instrument to exercise control over oil-producing countries in West Africa. Certain of Yar'Adua's advisors played a key role in the development of Nigeria's foreign policy in the 1970s.[98]

The first weeks of August 2023 were a veritable obstacle course for the CNSP. Not only did it demonstrate nerves of steel and unfailing determination in the face of Western sanctions and invasion threats from ECOWAS, but it rapidly formed its first transition government cabinet, which led to intense activity on the side of the people. On August 13, Niger's transition government was visited by religious leaders from Northern Nigeria whose historic ties with the people of southern Niger are a guarantee of support for Niger. Fortunately, Niger has enjoyed the Pan-African solidarity of the fraternal peoples of Burkina Faso and Mali. For example, on August 21, 2023, in response to the sanctions against the people of Niger, the government of Burkina Faso sent a convoy of 311 trucks with tons of provisions to supply the Nigerien population with basic necessities. Representatives from Mali and Burkina Faso made public statements of their unconditional support and the special intervention forces of these two countries have agreed to meet in Niger to train the army in the event that France does unleash a war.

Following the referendum of June 18, the Constitutional Council of Mali approved a new constitution. Assimi Goita, Mali's president during the transition period, confronted the same sanctions and threats currently levied against Nigeriens. In January 2022, ECOWAS lifted its economic and financial sanctions against Mali in exchange for the scheduling of elections. However, the following July, the US Treasury Department imposed new sanctions against Mali's transition government and various military leaders, including Defense Secretary Sadio Camara, for having "worked closely with the Wagner Group to facilitate and expand Wagner's presence in Mali."[99]

The will of the new governments to renegotiate the contracts is an encouraging sign, and hopefully leads to the increase of the prices of raw commodities. The days of constantly falling prices are over! Moreover, sanctions have obliged Mali, Burkina Faso, and Niger to accelerate their efforts to strengthen their sovereignty. In March 2023, Mali approved financing for the construction of a gold refinery with a planned monthly production capacity of twenty tons. Gold mining in Mali covers 25 percent of the national budget and accounts for 75 percent of export earnings. Niger, which is Africa's third-largest gold producer after Ghana and South Africa, also has iron ore, manganese, and lithium reserves. Its amended mining code, adopted in August 2023, allows for state participation in new mining projects of up to 30 percent. While this amended mining code includes provisions for creating various funds, it also lifts exemptions applicable to the production of petroleum products.

In Burkina Faso as well, the construction of a gold refinery is a priority and the relevant legislation is being drafted to that end. In July 2023, Burkina Faso passed a law to amend the mining code of 2015. Under this new law, a 17 billion CFA franc Patriotic Support Fund (FSP) was established. In addition, a Local Development Mining Fund (FMDL) was created to establish "funding for regional and district development plans."[100] Finally, under an agreement signed with Iran's Minister of Oil, a crude oil refinery will be built, which will enable the country to secure its energy supply and resist sanctions. In exchange, Burkina Faso may grant mining concessions to Iran.[101]

On the other hand, there are worrying signs of Western duplicity. After a meeting between members of the CNSP and a representative of the French army, who gave assurances that France would begin withdrawing its troops, the CNSP issued a communiqué in early September 2023 denouncing suspicious troop movements in neighboring countries. Given the CNSP's popular support, a Western destabilization operation that doesn't entail mobilizing foreign occupation forces would be more likely to succeed.

Neocolonialists are very likely considering various scenarios for Niger. In scenario number one, they would, with the support of Tuareg secessionists, fracture Niger along the lines of past such attempts in Mali, Nigeria, or more recently, in northern Ethiopia. On August 9, 2023, ex-Tuareg rebel Rhissa Ag Boula announced the formation of an armed struggle movement named *La Résistance*, which appears to confirm this approach. However, the fact that such groups enjoy little or no support within the Tuareg population represents a problem. Under scenario number two, a "surgical military operation" or a series of covert operations would be carried out to eliminate the CNSP and its main support base. In scenario number three, the neocolonialists would provide material, financial, and operational support to terrorist groups in order to destabilize Niger and allied countries. These scenarios may, of course, also be mixed and matched.

The coup in Niger also represents a chess move to save and protect the ongoing Pan-African revolutionary process in neighboring countries. According to Roland

Diagne Fodé, a Senegalese and Pan-African activist, Bazoum made the mistake of welcoming former terrorists into his supposed deradicalization program. That was a mistake because he risked discrediting himself in terms of the official "anti-terrorist" strategy. In his analysis of a March 2022 Agence France Presse article entitled "Niger is moving towards peace by maintaining conversations with jihadis," Diagne observes that:

> . . . this article contains troubling details about the new policy implemented by the Nigerien president in this regard. He states that he freed several militants and received them in the presidential palace. In 2016, when he was the Interior Minister, he managed to get dozens of Boko Haram jihadis from south eastern Niger to enroll in a program that combined deradicalization with job training (. . .) The government has also been in contact with Jama'at Nusrat al-Islam wal-Muslimin (Group for the Support of Islam and Muslims—JNIM), a coalition affiliated with Al Qaeda (. . .)[102]

Diagne then cites another source, according to whom JNIM commanders:

> . . . send messages saying "we won't attack you if you don't attack us." The Group also asked the government to free certain prisoners, which was done.

According to Diagne:

. . . it's irrefutable that Bazoum received an order from his Western masters to ally with Al Qaeda and ISIS, thereby allowing those two organizations to use Niger as a base to destabilize the patriotic military juntas of Mali and Burkina Faso, as part of the West's proxy war against Russia.[103]

One of the CNSP's very first communiqués denounced the French army's liberation of a dozen terrorists in Niger (Paris immediately denied this allegation). On September 7, 2023, a terrorist rocket attack took place against a passenger ship of the Malian Shipping Company on the Niger River in the Timbuktu region, which attested to the barbarity that the terrorist threat represents in the region. Deemed "a war crime" by the International Federation for Human Rights, nearly one hundred persons, mostly civilians, were killed in this massacre. The Group for the Support of Islam and Muslims (JNIM) claimed responsibility for the rocket attack.

On September 16, 2023, the leaders of the military juntas of Mali, Burkina Faso, and Niger, Assimi Goita, Ibrahim Touré, and Abdourahamane Tiani, respectively, announced the creation of the Alliance of Sahel States. In so doing, they struck a blow against foreign interference and took a step forward in confronting their enemies, both within and beyond their countries' borders. This action also clearly demonstrates how to build Pan-African unity: Africans must think in terms of their own interests rather than submit to old or new masters.

CONCLUSION

Today, solidarity with the Nigerien people is an important contribution to the cause of humanity and the cause of peoples struggling against the crimes of colonialism. Although there is more to neocolonial domination than the presence of foreign military bases, the expulsion of the French, European and American military is a sine qua non of true national independence.

The transition government in Niger created a huge stir with its 180-degree turn. However, in this it had been preceded by other African countries, of which little is heard, such as Eritrea, a young nation, which emerged out of an armed liberation struggle against the Ethiopian regime and achieved victory after a twenty-nine-year war of liberation that culminated in the referendum of April 1993.

How has Eritrea fared?

After its hard-earned independence, conquered without assistance from great powers, Eritrea set itself the goal of autocentric development. For a country of the Global South, although elections held under a sword of Damocles may not be a priority, national development, on the other hand, is absolutely a priority. The same is true for self-reliance, which Eritrea ensured by endowing its people with both political consciousness and military training.

During the era of anti-colonial struggle, the African peoples could count on Soviet support and cooperation in the form of economic agreements with the USSR. In 1965, in a celebrated speech in Algiers, Che Guevara demanded that the socialist countries provide their firm and unconditional assistance to countries struggling for their national liberation. In those days, Pan-African unity was not sufficient—if it had been, then the peoples of Africa could indeed have triumphed without external assistance. However, in that era, their enemies were still too powerful. Victories and defeats do not depend solely on people's determination: one lives and struggles under conditions that are not of one's choosing.

Those who see the Russian or Chinese presence in Africa as comparable to Western imperialism fail to consider an important difference: cooperation with Russia and China is based on respectful relations. For example, in 2021, Eritrea signed an agreement to participate in the Belt and Road Initiative and, as a result, is able to plan infrastructure, telecommunications, mining, agriculture, and fisheries projects thanks to Chinese capital. In addition, China financed a five-hundred-kilometer highway project between the ports of Assab and Massawa. And yet, the government of Eritrea is usually considered one of the least open in the world due to its rejection of "international aid" institutions, so-called NGOs, and Western multinationals.

The Pan-African revolutionary governments should follow Eritrea's example and carefully scrutinize and reject Western "NGO-ization," which results in the tutelage of so-called civil society and indirect control by imperialism. The US Agency for International Development (USAID), the National Endowment for Democracy (NED), and other foundations must be considered neocolonial Trojan horses. CIA spies and their analogues from other countries use humanitarian aid as a cover to carry out and hide multiple crimes. In 1991, in a statement that should be taken at face value, no less a personage than former NED head Allen Weinstein stated that "a lot of what we do today was done covertly twenty-five years ago by the CIA."[104] Translation: Vigilance has diminished among the defenders of national sovereignty in the Global South who allow "friends" in the guise of humanitarian workers to spy on them and destroy their countries from within.

As the recent case of Ethiopia shows, it's important to combat secessionist movements supported by NATO countries. The US acts in far more discreet ways than France, but, as an actor in the shadows, it is capable of changing things in unexpected ways. In North Africa for example, Trump's support for Morocco's takeover of Western Sahara has had considerable consequences in the region. In particular, it brought to light Morocco's relations with Zionism, which were presented under the propagandistic guise of interreligious friendship in order to hide the crimes against the Palestinian people.

Many Africans also remember the war in Libya. At the time, the Obama administration took care to remain in the shadows. However, after Qadafi was brutally lynched and assassinated, Secretary of State Hillary Clinton could not contain herself when, upon arriving at the scene of the crime, she crowed: "We came, we saw, he died." American think tanks know full well that a change in strategic vision is required:

> . . . concerns for democracy and African economic emergencies were never a priority

[for the US]; we even saw autocratic regimes receive quiet support on the grounds that they were anti-communist or aiding in the fight against terrorism. This simplistic approach has done much to weaken the position of the West in Africa. (. . .) Today, double talk and double standards are tolerated less and less and encounter increased scrutiny from young Africans who are quick to mobilize through social media.[105]

Finally, Pan-Africanism can wage decisive battles provided it comes to the assistance of countries attacked or destabilized by Western sponsored wars. If Africa is to escape the economic domination of the IMF and the World Bank, the debt must be canceled and funding provided for regional unity projects that facilitate cooperation between fraternal peoples. Economic modernization and diversification must allow the working masses to gain access to better living conditions. The African peoples have stood up, are on the march, and are ready to fight. International solidarity, also known as the debt we owe humanity, plays a necessary role as well. The prose of Cuba's Liberator José Martí, so often brimming with revolutionary fervor, pointed the way to this noble objective in these simple words: " . . . peoples who are presently unacquainted must rush to know each other like the brothers in arms they are fated to be."[106]

AFTERWORD TO THE US EDITION

Many of the events that unfolded in the early months of the new military transition government in Niger are recounted in these pages. Written during the weeks after the CNSP took power, this essay was published just three months later, on the occasion of the Venezuela International Book Fair (Filven 2023). Nicolás Maduro, the president of the Bolivarian Republic of Venezuela, officially introduced it with the following words: "It's a provocative book on a hot topic for geopolitical thinkers." News of this new US edition is an even greater honor, if that's possible. It's fitting that a book inspired by the words of José Martí is now available to the American people whose contribution to Pan-Africanism was so decisive for millions of Africans. I trust that this study will serve to consolidate the existing bonds of brotherhood between the peoples of the Sahel and the American people. From now on, knowledge of Niger's contemporary history will be intimately connected with the current fight against imperialism in a—until recently—forgotten region. As with past struggles against colonialism, the defeat of French and American imperialism in Niger is seen as a universal victory of peoples in struggle.

Who, in its early days, bet on the mettle and steadfast character of this revolution, supposedly led by a "vulgar military junta"? One thing is certain: the assumptions of the dominant media were imbued with Eurocentrism, a toxic legacy of colonialism in Africa. From the very outset, the mainstream media fully bought into the assumption that the CNSP government had little future and propagated the most facile and crude propaganda memes. Consequently, not only did the media blunder in their predictions, but in so doing they permanently discredited themselves, thereby accelerating the radicalization of the Pan-African Revolution. The mainstream media's clear bias in favor of destabilization and neocolonial interference was such that the Nigerien people not only came to a better understanding of who said media are, but they also grasped how their historic enemies really act.

The arguments advanced in my book required validation through an analysis of subsequent events. First of all, it was essential to drive home the point that the new government carried out a coup to recover Niger's national sovereignty, which president Bazoum had surrendered to France for a pittance. It was also important to consider that the coup didn't spill a drop of blood and enjoyed the people's support from the beginning. The most important point was that the people remained active protagonists and, consequently, the defense of national sovereignty took the form of a united civilian-military force capable of responding to the many challenges that arose. As a result, rather than devolve into a *"vulgar military junta,"* the leaders of the CNSP became decisive actors in a new chapter of African history. Following the CNSP's arrival in power, the policies of France, the European Union, the United States of America, and the World Bank had a common denominator: the recourse to blackmail, up to and including threatening Niger with war. What they didn't expect was that, in the face of sanctions and blackmail, the Nigerien people and the CNSP would become even more resolute. The Nigerien people's regular mobilizations in support of the CNSP demonstrate that the hopes placed in the recovery of true national sovereignty are being crowned with success. As proof, one need only cite a series of events, which, taken together, attest to the invincible logic of the CNSP government's actions and to its observance of the promises made to the people.

In the initial post-coup period, various cynical protagonists took the stage, one of whom was revealed to the entire world when Niger, Mali, and Burkina Faso made the decision to leave ECOWAS, definitively and irreversibly, on January 28, 2024.[107] After so many insolent and barely veiled declarations of war, why then did ECOWAS end up lifting its sanctions against Niger on February 24, 2024?[108] What caused ECOWAS, which had been arrogantly flexing its muscles in the face of a clutch of defiant soldiers, to deflate like a balloon at a child's birthday party? First of all, the effects of the blockade against Niger, particularly in relation to electricity, were lessened with the commissioning of the thirty-megawatt Gorou Banda photovoltaic power plant on November 25, 2023.[109] Likewise, both Prime Minister Ali Lamine Zeine's successful state visits to Russia, Turkey, and Iran, as well as the "Access to the Atlantic Initiative," approved in Morocco with positive impacts on the countries of the Sahel, had the effect of countering the policy of isolating the Sahel, followed by the West African governments that are vassals of France. Finally, let's not forget that ECOWAS' defeat may also be attributed to Niger's clear strategic vision, based on the construction of Pan-African unity. In this regard, the visionary policy of former President Mamadou Tandja, who, in February 2010, approved the construction of the SORAZ oil refinery in Zinder, with Chinese financing, played an important role in strengthening sovereignty and energy cooperation. On February 17, 2024, a "Memorandum of Agreement on Gasoil Supply"[110] was signed in Niamey by Mali, Burkina Faso, Chad, and Togo, with the object of lessening their energy dependency. Likewise, Mali and Niger signed an important bilateral gasoil supply contract. According to the Oil Minister of Niger, Mahaman Moustapha Barké Bako, President Tiani gave very clear instructions: *"Try to apply preferential pricing, especially for AES countries."*[111] The partnership agreement signed on April 16, 2024, envisages the sale of 150 million liters of Nigerien gasoil to Mali, for 42 billion CFA francs, which will ensure *"fuel supplies to the country's different power plants."*[112]

Perhaps the most spectacular event—and greatest reason for celebration by the Nigerien people—was the expulsion of the French troops and the closing of their military base in Niamey, in compliance with the December 13, 2023 deadline. Not only that, but the CNSP also demanded that these troops be redeployed to Chad, instead of Benin, its neighbor to the South, as was originally intended. Also spectacular was the case of Sylvain Itté, the former French ambassador who, despite being declared "persona non grata," refused to leave Niger. In effect, Itté was forced to hide several weeks in a French embassy under siege by the local population, until he left the country clandestinely, like a thief in the night. He wrote an "I-was-there" book, scheduled for publication on March 13, 2024, which, however, the French Ministry of Foreign Affairs decreed *"unfit for publication."* The publishing house's copies were seized in their entirety and promotion of the book, which had already begun, was subject to a full censorship order. What a delicious irony, given France's supposed role as the great advocate of democracy in Africa! Anne-Marie Descôtes, Secretary General of the Ministry of Europe and Foreign Affairs, gave the reasons for this censorship in a letter, as follows:

> There's much information on France's crisis management system, your communications with the French authorities and Nigerien actors, the role, motivations and personalities of your interlocutors and, more generally, the conduct of our foreign policy. These, in some instances, are sensitive matters and, as you are the author, they are liable to be perceived as expressions of the point of view of the Government of France. It seems to me that this book project presents more risks than advantages in terms of our communications goals.[113]

All of this only confirmed the French ambassador's real sin: revealing too much about France's destabilization strategy in Niger. Shortly before France made its *"communications policy ruling,"* the CNSP authorities made public the discovery of a secret arms cache at the Sahel bureau of the European Union Capacity Building Mission (EUCAP-Sahel), an EU security and crisis management agency, which led to its expulsion from Niger in December. The scenes filmed by Nigerien national television not only showed ultramodern military equipment, but also maps of the country marked with strategic objectives, as well as a mysterious slogan in French: *"Peace: we can avoid it."* A motto more befitting of lumpen mafiosos than of security professionals.

After the public revelation of the roles played by so many dishonest actors in Niger, what more could be expected? As I've said many times, what one may expect from this Pan-African Revolution is . . . the very best! On March 16, 2024, after meeting with US officials, the CNSP slammed the door in the face of the US empire itself by announcing the termination of the security agreement of 2012, which served as the dubious legal basis for stationing US troops in Niger. US imperialist strategy in the region suffered a major blow with the closing of Air Base 101 in Niamey and, especially, the highly strategic Air Base 201 (the drones base) in Agadez, built at a cost of $110 million. Finally, this will also force the closing of a secret CIA base, in Dirkou, supposedly established to combat *"islamist insurgents"* in Libya,[114] according to the explanations given after its existence was revealed in 2018.

Demonstrating its long-term vision, the CNSP promptly took other measures, which will soon have a decisive impact. For example, in its economic policy, it revoked the agreement between France and Niger that proscribed double taxation, thereby striking a serious blow against a neocolonial system based on exorbitant privileges, which the presence of multinationals and French *"expats"* made so *"natural."* However, the most decisive action, one announced unambiguously, is the coming exit of Niger, Mali, and Burkina Faso from the CFA franc currency area. This policy was once instituted on a temporary basis in Mali, under President Modibo Keita. This time, however, the change may be definitive, given that it is premised on the joint exit of a bloc of countries, namely the AES and perhaps Senegal as well. This action would enable an authentic transformation of West Africa, under the leadership of Pan-African revolutionaries.

It seems to me that the story of Niger's struggle against imperialism is worth knowing. The Nigerien people have the right to dream and to glimpse a horizon of peace with the right to development. Words can inspire action. President Tiani chose the following words to explain the CNSP transition government's mission: our objective is to transform the Sahel from *"a zone of insecurity into a zone of prosperity."*

— Casablanca, April 20, 2024

POSTSCRIPT: YEAR ONE OF THE NIGERIEN REVOLUTION, CREATION OF THE ALLIANCE OF SAHEL STATES (AES)

This book has had an unexpected publication history. In a few months, the book the reader is holding in her hands has been—or will soon be—published in five countries: Spain, Venezuela, Cuba, the United States, and Niger. Published simultaneously in Spain and Venezuela in November 2023, the book's original premise was to serve as an introduction to the CNSP and its struggle in Niger, intended mainly for the Spanish-speaking African diaspora and lovers of justice in search of the truth, amid intense media propaganda campaigns. My Spanish and Venezuelan editors took the brave decision to publish the first book written on this topic. I delivered the manuscript early on September 16, 2023, which, as it happened, was the very day of the founding of the *Alliance of Sahel States*, an event that validates the book's thesis: we are living in an age of Pan-African Revolution. In the following months, various events offered further support for this thesis, even as increasing numbers of international observers began writing about and reporting on the transformations under way in the Sahel. The speeches and declarations of President Ibrahim Traoré of Burkina Faso, who is seen as a modern-day incarnation of Thomas Sankara, have probably greatly contributed to raising awareness of the objectives defended by the patriotic militaries of the Sahel.

A book is also a publishing venture and, as such, a gamble dependent on a favorable context or, in capitalist terms, on "the market." In the case of my book, it should be said, this was a secondary consideration. My Spanish publisher acceded to my request that should an interest in publishing the book arise in certain countries (in the Sahel, Cuba, etc.), the translation rights would then be granted to enable the widest possible access to information about the processes under way in the Sahel. This request took into account the context affecting publishers in many countries of the Global South, which, due to neocolonialism, are dependent on fragile structures. For instance, in many French-speaking African countries, there exists a tradition where the author pays the publisher to have his book published. The retail price of such books is sky high. Thus, whereas the argument that convinces the publisher is the one that fills his own pocket, knowledge is, however, never made accessible to the people with empty pockets. The contrast with the decolonizing cultural policy of Cuba and Venezuela could hardly be starker. During my stay in Caracas, I discovered, to my utter delight and surprise as an avid reader, the range of ambitious publications available there at very low prices. As a professor and educator, I hope that the countries of the Sahel adopt this approach, an approach that depends on resolving the problems of security and development.

I am writing these lines in the wake of two momentous events. On July 6, 2024, Burkina, Mali, and Niger signed the Confederation Treaty, thereby creating the Alliance of Sahel States, as an "intermediate stage to a [Sahel] Federation," in the words of Nigerien President Brigadier General Abdourahamane Tiani. On July 26, 2024, Nige-

riens celebrated the first anniversary of the CNSP's revolution. This celebration displaced the traditional observance of Niger's Independence Day on August 3. Said
date was instead officially renamed National Arbor Day
to underline concern over the consequences of climate
change in a region regularly stricken by droughts and
demonstrate the CNSP authorities' determination to
combat desertification.

In this brief text, it's probably not possible to explain
the extent to which the events in recent months have val-
idated my expectations and those of the peoples of the
Sahel. In fact, in recent months, crystal-clear answers have
emerged concerning many of the questions, hypotheses,
and uncertainties voiced in this book. I can only say that
the vision espoused by leaders like Assimi Goita, Abdourahamane Tiani, and Ibrahim Traoré is authentically revolutionary and, as such, reflects the desires and hopes of
the peoples of the Sahel. Tiani, for instance, expressed his
strategic vision in a widely disseminated document, which
outlined four strategic areas of action and focused on
popular education. In today's societies, where the media
is such a dominant force, President Tiani stands out as a
figure that makes few public statements and has no time
for idle chatter and vain polemics. When he expressed his
ideas, on the ideal occasion of the first anniversary of the
Revolution, it was obvious to the peoples of the Sahel and
the world that Tiani is endowed with the qualities of a
great and historic anti-imperialist leader.

The fight against neocolonialism, which these leaders
are waging today, was examined by Kwame Nkrumah,
who bequeathed us with many valuable reflections:

> Coups d'état are expressions of the class
> struggle and the struggle between imperial-

ism and socialist revolution. (. . .) the army is not merely an instrument in the struggle, but becomes itself part of the class struggle, thus tearing down the artificial wall separating it from the socioeconomic and political transformations in society.

In Niger, a country particularly beset by many of the contradictions of neocolonialism, the CNSP has acted decisively. And it has done so in record time, in accordance with the aspirations of an entire people. However, it's no longer the history of a single country that must be known and studied, but rather that of an African Federation in gestation, which is following the path of thinkers and founding fathers like Nkrumah. That's the subject of my next book, which I am cowriting with a Cameroonian author.

—*Barcelona, August 8, 2024*

ENDNOTES

Introduction

1   See Institut National de la Statistique du Niger, *Stat-Niger*.

2   Africanews Editorial Staff and AFP, "Ces Maliens qui refont leur vie au Niger pour fuir le terrorisme," *Africanews*, February 15, 2022.

3   "Il ne faut pas oublier les réfugiés au Niger, il ne faut pas oublier le Sahel," *ONU Info*, April 19, 2021.

4   *Global Multidimensional Poverty Index 2023—Unstacking global poverty: Data for high-impact action*, United Nations Development Programme (UNDP) and Oxford Poverty and Human Development Initiative, 2023.

5   Liza Fabbian, "Le Niger et le Nigeria, deux pays et deux populations intimement liés," *RFI*, August 7, 2023.

6   "Niger Economic Outlook," *African Development Bank Group*. afdb.org.

7   Thomas Sankara, "Il faut annuler la dette—29 juillet, 1987, sommet de l'OUA Addis Abéba," *Thomassankara.net*.

8   Founded in 1975, ECOWAS purports to represent the economic interests of the countries of West Africa. It consisted of fourteen members—Benin, Cape Verde, Gambia, Ghana, Guinea, Guinea-Bissau, Liberia, Senegal, Mali, Burkina Faso, Niger, Nigeria, Sierra Leona, and Togo—before this number fell to eleven countries.

**Chapter 1: From the French Intervention in Mali
to the Coup in Niger**

9   "Les explications du premier ministre Choguel Kokalla Maiga concernant la venue de Wagner," *Quotidien du Mali*, September 18, 2021 and Sylvère Dossou, "Mali - Affaire Wagner: 'il faut qu'on ait la possibilité de regarder vers d'autres horizons,'" *L'Événement Niger*, September 20, 2021.

10   "Mali : Macron qualifie de 'honte' les propos du Premier ministre sur un 'abandon' par la France," *France24*, October 1, 2021.

11   Aminata Traoré, Boubacar Boris Diop, et al, "Appel pour une coalition des intellectuel-le-s et des artistes pour une paix durable, la sécurité humaine et la préservation de l'environnement," *Investig'action*, March 13, 2020. https://investigaction-net. translate.goog/crises-au-sahel-faire-taire-les-armes-pas-les-peuples/?_x_tr_sl=fr&_x_tr_tl=en&_x_tr_hl=en&_x_tr_pto=sc

12   Bruno Jaffré, "Octobre 2022, coup d'État, insurrection . . . le Burkina rabat ses cartes," blog post on *Le Club de Mediapart*, October 14, 2022.

13   Ibid.

14   Laurie Fachaux, "Mali : 'L'arrivée de l'armée à Kidal est acceptée et négociée depuis des mois,'" *TV5MONDE*, December 24, 2021.

15   Ibid.

16   Martin Mateso, "Mali: la peur de l'insécurité alimente le syndrome d'une partition du pays," *FranceInfo*, December 5, 2017.

17   Eléonore Abou Ez, "Le terrorisme a fait plus de 4000 morts en 2019 dans le Sahel," *FranceInfo*, January 10, 2020.

18   Franck Cognard, "'Nous évitons le pire': au Sahel, le chef de l'armée française réaffirme la nécessité de l'opération Barkhane," *FranceInfo*, December 16, 2019.

19   Thierry Oberlé, "Aqmi épaule les rebelles touaregs," *Le Figaro*, March 14, 2012.

20   "La France nous avait donné son feu vert pour l'indépendance de l'Azawad," *Le Courrier du Sahara*, April 9, 2015. https:// investigaction.net/la-france-nous-avait-donne-son-feu/

21   UNHCR Global Report 2022. https://reporting.unhcr.org/ global-report-2022

22 World Nuclear Association, "World Uranium Mining Production," World Nuclear Association, May 16, 2024, https://world-nuclear. org/information-library/nuclear-fuel-cycle/mining-of-uranium/ world-uranium-mining-production.

Chapter 2: The Errors of French Interference in the Sahel

23 "Projet de loi n° 226 autorisant l'approbation de l'accord de défense conclu le 24 avril 1961 entre les Gouvernements de la République française, de la République de Côte-d'Ivoire, de la République du Dahomey et de la République du Niger." https://www.senat.fr/ leg/1960-1961/i1960_1961_0226.pdf

24 Thomas Borrel, Thomas Deltombe, et al, *L'empire qui ne veut pas mourir: une histoire de la Françafrique* (Paris: Éditions du Seuil, 2021), 379.

25 "Assassinat de S. Olympio, ancien pdt du Togo: les archives françaises peuvent-elles parler ?" *RFI*, January 13, 2023. https:// www.youtube.com/watch?v=IjhNMdLoLMQ

26 Roger Coindreau and Charles Penz, Le Maroc: *Maroc français, Maroc espagnol, Tanger* (Paris: Société d'Éditions Géographiques, Maritimes et Coloniales, 1949), 100.

27 Pierre Singaravélou (ed.), *Les empires coloniaux XIX–XX siècle* (Paris: Éditions Point, 2013).

28 Ibid.

29 Thomas Deltombe, Manuel Domergue and Jacob Tatsitsa, *Kamerun! Une guerre cachée aux origines de la Françafrique, 1948– 1971* (Paris: La Découverte, 2018), 409.

30 The Economic and Social Development Fund, an institution created by France in 1946 to plan investments in the African continent.

31 Thomas Borrel, *L'empire qui ne veut pas mourir*, 299.

32 Ibid, 327.

33 Ibid.

34 Jean Ziegler (with the collaboration of Laurence Lomme), *La Terre qu'on a : Luttes et Défaites du Tiers Monde* (Paris: Études et Documentation Internationales, 1989), 80.

35 Thomas Deltombe, Manuel Domergue and Jacob Tatsitsa, *Kamerun!*, 778.

36   Rahmane Idrissa, "Rule by Junta," *Sidecar (New Left Review* blog), August 7, 2023.

37   Ibid.

38   "Le Niger débordé par le terrorisme djihadiste," *Le Point*, March 23, 2021.

Chapter 3: Niger: Under the Heel of Servitude and Neoliberalism

39   The Energy and Oil Ministry of Niger, *Électrification rurale et accès des ruraux aux services énergétiques modernes: analyse de contexte et proposition de cadres et outils de gouvernance sectorielle* (UNDP, Global Environment Facility, and Republic of Niger: 2016), 11. https://erc.undp.org/api/d?filePath=%2Fdocuments%2F7169%2F mgmtresponse%2Fkeyaction%2Fdoc_4393155305759759086PR ASE1.pdf

40   Ibid.

41   Ibid.

42   Ibid, 10.

43   Ibid, 12.

44   Ibid, 2.

45   Ibid, 3.

46   Ibid, 4.

47   Ibid, 18.

48   *Rapport   RSE   de   Bolloré   Logistics*, accessed on August   25,   2023.   https://www.bollore-logistics. com/app/assets-bollorelgs/uploads/2021/07/ rapport_rse_bollore_logistics_2020_2021_fr.pdf.

49   "Train entre Niamey et Cotonou: Bolloré débouté par la justice béninoise," *France 24*, October 4, 2017.

50   Rémi Carayol, "Bolloré, un empire françafricain (3): Au Niger et au Bénin, le train fantôme de Bolloré," *Afrique XXI*, March 2, 2022.

51   Ibid.

52   Ministère du Plan - République du Niger, *Plan de Développement Économique et Social 2017–2021.*

53   World Bank, *https://www.banquemondiale.org/fr/country/niger/ overview (accessed September 1, 2023).*

Chapter 4: Raw Materials: The Story Behind the Story

54 See: l'Union Monétaire Ouest Africaine (UMOA)-Titres, "Note d'information: République du Nigerpdes," December 2019, https://www.umoatitres.org/wp-content/uploads/2020/01/Note-dinformation-Niger-2019-1.pdf; and l'Union Monétaire Ouest Africaine (UMOA)-Titres, "Note d'information – République du Niger," *WATHI* (blog), December 16, 2020, https://www.wathi.org/wathinote-election-niger-situation-economie/note-dinformation-republique-du-niger-umoa-titres/.

55 See: Elikia M'Bokolo, *L'Afrique au XX siècle : Le continent convoité* (Paris: Éditions Points, 1985).

56 See footnote no. 4.

57 Youssoufou Hamadou Daouda, "Responsabilité sociétale des multinationales en Afrique Subsaharienne : enjeux et controverses—Cas du groupe Areva au Niger," *Vertigo* 14, no. 1 (2014): 7. https://www.erudit.org/fr/revues/vertigo/2014-v14-n1-vertigo01649/1027967ar/.

58 Ibid.

59 Ibid, 8.

60 "Le directeur du groupe nucléaire français Areva a été expulsé," *RFI*, July 26, 2007. http://www1.rfi.fr/actufr/articles/091/article_54512.asp.

61 Freddie Ponton, "'Uraniumgate'—The Futility of Fighting Corruption in Neocolonial Africa," *21st Century Wire*, August 9, 2023. https://21stcenturywire.com/2023/08/09/niger-uraniumgate-futility-of-fighting-corruption-in-neocolonial-africa/.

62 Vincent Caupin, *Les flux d'hydrocarbures entre le Niger et le Nigéria : formes, estimation, déterminants et impact sur l'économie du Niger* (Paris: Institut de Institut français de recherche scientifique pour le développement en coopération, 1997), 10. https://horizon.documentation.ird.fr/exl-doc/pleins_textes/divers15-06/010027092.pdf

63 Ibid, 12.

64 Ibid, 21.

65 Moussa Naganou, "La mission stratégique de la Sonidep compromise !," *Niger diaspora*, June 16, 2012.

66 Omar Hamidou Tchiana, Assemblée nationale—Question d'actualité au Ministre du Pétrole, June 11, 2022. https://www.facebook.com/o/?fbid=543424780621023&set=a.165475695082602&locale=ms_MY

67 Ibid.

68 Ibid.

69 "'Arrêtez de boire de l'eau puisqu'elle est européenne' : l'ambassadeur français au Niger s'excuse," *Spoutnik Afrique*, February 13, 2023. https://fr.sputniknews.africa/20230213/-arretez-de-boire-de-leau-puisquelle-est-europeenne-lambassadeur-francais-au-niger-sexcuse-1057908483.html

70 [Author's updated note] The Veolia contract of water production and distribution in Niger by the French has been rescinded by the CNSP as of the end of 2023. In fact, the end of the contract was already decided by Bazoum's government in October 2022. That decision was followed by negotiations so that Veolia could keep its activities, but the state's authorities were opposed to it. As the contract was finishing on December 31, the CNSP made their final decision, taking into account the many criticisms of Veolia privatization of Nigerien water for the past twenty years. See: Koami Agbetiafa, "Reprise du contrat d'affermage de la SEEN : L'État oppose son veto," Nigerinter, October 19, 2022, https://nigerinter.com/2022/10/19/reprise-du-contrat-daffermage-de-la-seen-letat-oppose-son-veto/

71 [Author's note as of August 2024] These figures are prior to 2020. Since then, daily oil production in Nigeria has declined considerably, from 2 million to the most recent figure of 1.3 million (December 2023). Niger's announced oil production would still be far behind. See: Abdel-Latif Boureima, "Nigéria : la production d'or noir a augmenté d'un peu plus de 7 % en décembre 2023," Agence Ecofin, January 18, 2024, https://www.agenceecofin.com/hydrocarbures/1801-115336-nigeria-la-production-d-or-noir-a-augmente-d-un-peu-plus-de-7-en-decembre-2023.

72 Laurent Ribadeau Dumas, "Maroc-Nigeria: un projet de gazoduc pour exporter le gaz jusqu'en Europe," *Franceinfo*, June 6, 2018. https://www.francetvinfo.fr/monde/afrique/politique-africaine/maroc-nigeria-un-projet-de-gazoduc-pour-exporter-du-gaz-jusquen-europe_3054331.html

Chapter 5: Russia Behind the Scenes: Myths and Realities

73 Sarah Daly, *Russia's influence in Africa, a security perspective* (Washington: Atlantic Council, 2023), 2. https://www. atlanticcouncil.org/in-depth-research-reports/report/ russias-influence-in-africa-a-security-perspective/.

74 Elikia M'Bokolo, *L'Afrique au XXe siècle*, 371.

75 Alex Anfruns, "Si l'Europe s'est développée, c'est à partir des richesses de l'Afrique," *Aujourd'hui l'Afrique* Special Issue on 60th Anniversary of African Independence (February 2020): 35. https://gresea.be/ Si-l-Europe-s-est-developpee-c-est-a-partir-des-richesses-de-l-Afrique

76 Ibid, 38.

77 Paul Bairoch, *Le tiers-monde dans l'impasse* (Paris: Gallimard, 1971), 118.

78 Ibid, 117.

79 Yash Tandon, *Trade is War: The West's War against the World* (New York: OR Books, 2018).

80 Alex Anfruns, "Coronavirus and Black Lives Matter is a double revolution that opens a possibility for Africa to change its relationship with the west", The Canary, July 21, 2020. https:// www.thecanary.co/global/2020/07/21/coronavirus-and-black-lives-matter-is-a-double-revolution-that-opens-a-possibility-for-africa-to-change-its-relationship-with-the-west/

81 Ibid.

82 Agnès Verdebout, *Ventes d'armes russes en Afrique : les effets contrariés des sanctions occidentales* (Brussels: Groupe de recherche et d'information sur la paix et la sécurité, 2023), 4. https://www. grip.org/wp-content/uploads/2023/05/NA_2023-05-31_FR_ AV-Armes-russes-Afrique.pdf.

83 Ibid, 5.

84 "États-Unis : 27 membres du Congrès américain réclament des sanctions contre l'Algérie," *Algérie Eco*, October 1, 2022. https:// www.algerie-eco.com/2022/10/01/etats-unis-27-membres-du-congres-americain-reclament-des-sanctions-contre-lalgerie/.

85 Verdebout (op. cit.) 7.

86 Ibid.

87 Olivier Ndekop, "Centrafrique : les raisons cachées de l'intervention française," *Institut Frantz Fanon*,

January   23,   2014.   https://institutfrantzfanon.org/centrafrique-les-raisons-cachees-de-lintervention-francaise/

88 Jean-Fernand Koena, "Cinq ans de présence russe en Centrafrique," *DW*, July 25, 2023. https://www.dw.com/fr/cinq-ans-de-presence-russe-centrafrique/a-66347287

89 Claire Meynial, "Boko Haram se nourrit de l'échec de l'État nigérian," *Le Point*, May 18, 2014. https://www.lepoint.fr/afrique/boko-haram-se-nourrit-de-l-echec-de-l-etat-nigerian-18-05-2014-1857919_3826.php

90 Ibid.

91 Ibid.

92 *Defense Fact Sheet* (Niamey: US Embassy in Niger, October 25, 2018). https://ne.usembassy.gov/wp-content/uploads/sites/56/2018-10-25_Defense-Fact-Sheet-French.pdf

Chapter 6: Pan-African Unity against Western Terrorism

93 "Tchad : un coup d'État institutionnel dénoncé par les principaux partis d'opposition," *TV5MONDE*, March 3, 2021.

94 Frantz Fanon, *Pour la révolution africaine* (Paris: La Découverte, 2001), 69. This quote is taken from the digital version of the book prepared by the University of Quebec in Chicoutimi. http://classiques.uqac.ca/classiques/fanon_franz/pour_une_revolution_africaine/pour_une_revolution_africaine.pdf

95 Viviane Forson, "Le Nigeria est véritablement à la croisée des chemins," *Le Point*, February 25, 2023. https://www.lepoint.fr/afrique/le-nigeria-est-veritablement-a-la-croisee-des-chemins-25-02-2023-2509971_3826.php

96 Borrel, Deltombe, et al (op. cit.), *L'Empire qui ne veut pas mourir*, 438.

97 Ike Okonta, "Nigeria's resurgent oil diplomacy," *Project Syndicate*, January 18, 2008. https://www.project-syndicate.org/commentary/nigeria-s-resurgent-oil-diplomacy

98 Ibid.

99 Anthony J. Blinken, "Imposing Sanctions on Malian Officials in Connection with the Wagner Group," US State Department press release, July 24, 2023.

100 Jean Narcisse Koudou, "Burkina Faso: Le code minier modifié pour intégrer le fonds de soutien patriotique," *Journal la Paix*, July 26, 2023.

101 Abdel-Latif Boureima, "Burkina Faso: l'Iran soutient l'nstallation d'une raffinerie de pétrole dans le pays," *Agence Ecofin*, September 8, 2023. https://www.agenceecofin.com/hydrocarbures/0809-111564-burkina-faso-l-iran-soutient-l-installation-d-une-raffinerie-de-petrole-dans-le-pays

102 Roland Diagne Fodé, "Coups d'État souverainistes au MALI, BURKINA, NIGER, et l'effondrement en cours de la Françafrique, l'Eurafrique et l'Usafrique," *Impact.sn*, August 21, 2023. https://www.impact.sn/Coups-d-Etat-souverainistes-au-MALI-BURKINA-NIGER-et-l-effondrement-en-cours-de-la-francafrique-l-eurafrique-et-l_a39763.html

103 Ibid.

Conclusion

104 David Ignatius, "Innocence abroad: the new world of spyless coups," *Washington Post*, September 22, 1991. https://bityl.co/Ld46

105 Sarah Daly, *Russia's influence in Africa, a security perspective*, 3.

106 José Martí, "Nuestra América." Available at www.josemarti.cu

Afterword to US Edition

107 "Le Burkina Faso, le Mali et le Niger annoncent leur retrait de la Cedeao" *Le Monde*, January 28, 2024. https://www.lemonde.fr/afrique/article/2024/01/28/le-burkina-faso-le-mali-et-le-niger-annoncent-leur-retrait-de-la-cedeao_6213540_3212.html

108 "Niger : la Cedeao lève une grande partie des sanctions prises après le coup d'Etat militaire," *Le Monde*, February 24, 2024. https://www.lemonde.fr/afrique/article/2024/02/24/niger-la-cedeao-leve-une-grande-partie-des-sanctions-prises-apres-le-coup-d-etat-militaire_6218384_3212.html

109 Almoustapha Aboubacar, "Inauguration de la centrale solaire de Gorou Banda : Le solaire comme solution au problème d'énergie électrique," *Niger inter*, December 4, 2023. https://nigerinter.com/2023/12/04/inauguration-de-la-centrale-solaire-

de-gorou-banda-le-solaire-comme-solution-au-probleme-denergie-electrique

110 "Coopération énergétique : le Niger va approvisionner quatre pays en gasoil," *Energies Media*, February 19, 2024. https://energies-media.com/cooperation-energe-le-niger-va-approvisionner-quatre-pays-en-gasoil

111 Hamissou Yahaya, "Pourparlers de contrat d'approvisionnement en gasoil entre le Niger et le Mali : Le Niger en voie de devenir fournisseur exclusif du Mali en produit pétrolier," *ONEP Niger*, March 5, 2024. https://www.lesahel.org/pourparlers-de-contrat-dapprovisionnement-en-gasoil-entre-le-niger-et-le-mali-le-niger-en-voie-de-devenir-fournisseur-exclusif-du-mali-en-produit--petrolier

112 Émilienne Compaoré, "Coopération : Le Mali obtient 150 millions de litres de gasoil du Niger," *Libreinfo*, April 17, 2024. https://libreinfo.net/burkinamali-niger-gasoil

113 Arnaud Amegan, "Niger : la parution du livre de Sylvain Itté interdite par les autorités françaises," *ToutAfrica*, February 25, 2024. https://www.toutafrica.com/2024/01/25/niger-la-parution-du-livre-de-sylvain-itte-interdite-par-les-autorites-francaises

114 Elizabeth Pierson, "Drones, base secrète de la CIA, millions de dollars d'aide . . . Pourquoi les Américains sont au premier plan au Niger," *Le Figaro*, August 8, 2023. https://www.lefigaro.fr/international/drones-base-secrete-de-la-cia-millions-de-dollars-d-aide-pourquoi-les-americains-sont-au-premier-plan-au-niger-20230808

www.ingramcontent.com/pod-product-compliance
Lightning Source LLC
Chambersburg PA
CBHW020415130626
46549CB00006B/2570